BEIRUT DIARY

SIS LEVIN

A Husband Held Hostage
and a Wife Determined
to Set Him Free

INTERVARSITY PRESS
DOWNERS GROVE, ILLINOIS 60515

Distributed in Canada through InterVarsity Press, 860 Denison St., Unit 3, Markham, Ontario L3R 4H1, Canada.

Cover illustration: Guy Wolek

ISBN 0-8308-1716-6

Printed in the United States of America ∞

Library of Congress Cataloging-in-Publication Data
Levin, Sis, 1931-
    Beirut diary : a husband held hostage and a wife determined to set
    him free / Sis Levin.
      p.   cm.
    ISBN 0-8303-1716-6
      1. Levin, Jerry—Captivity, 1984.   2. Levin, Sis, 1931-
  —Journeys—Syria.   3. Levin, Sis, 1931- —Relations with hostages.
  4. Hostages—Lebanon.   5. Hostages—United States.   6. Syria—
  Foreign relations.   I. Title.
  DS87.2.L48L48   1989
956.9104'2'0922—dc20

89-19750
CIP

---

16   15   14   13   12   11   10   9   8   7   6   5   4   3   2   1
99   98   97   96   95   94   93   92   91   90   89

The book is, of course,
dedicated to Jerry
With whom I've shared the struggle
for faith,
From whom I've learned the lessons
of hope,
But, most of all, the one whom
I simply love.

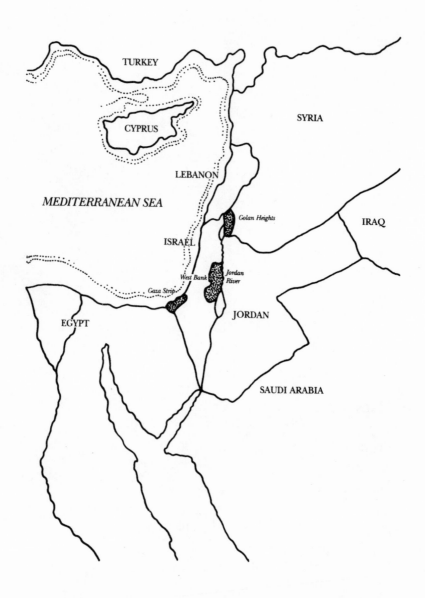

MIDDLE EAST

Preface

A teacher named William Bigelow began teaching a unit on South Africa two years after the Soweto uprising. Feeling he needed more appropriate material, he wrote his own: *Strangers in Their Own Country*. In his opening statements, Bigelow says: "There is no more a 'black problem' than Nazi Germany had been a 'Jewish problem.' "[1]

Motivated by little knowledge beyond the American press, Bigelow realized:

> The situation created by the oppressive apartheid system was a civil war waiting to happen. . . . [The] deepening U.S. involvement complicated this ominous future [and] still more worrisome was evidence that South Africa had the capability to explode nuclear weapons.[2]

I firmly believe that the Israeli-Palestinian conflict fits this description. I too feel deeply that this is not only a "Jewish-Arab" problem; it is the world's problem and for the very reasons Bigelow states. Certainly, if the moral demands of this issue escape us, then the practical ones won't . . . finally.

The nuclear capability is there, and the rage and panic are fully capable of igniting that "final solution" and involving us irreversibly and permanently.

Bigelow wanted his students to know that "change was possible; perhaps [his book] could even offer them an opportunity to play a small part in creating that change."[3] Our children, our students, have at least a right to know the facts about this moment in history, including the hope that they can, as Bigelow says, "play a small part" in determining how this problem, our problem, is resolved.

There was a time when I would have preferred *not* to become involved. I am a lover, not a fighter. And, furthermore, I have always been afraid of conflict. In matters of "fight or flight," I have always run.

As my diary records, I was drawn unwillingly into a place where, if I ran away, I would lose that one whom I loved more than myself. Forced to stay, I learned that in spite of my fears, I could "play a small part." That is what I want to teach now and hope to be able to "show and tell" through this book.

My heart is full of thanks to the God who sustained me; the Episcopal church in Birmingham, Alabama, which first taught me (under a truly great bishop, Bill Stough) about being a "blessed peacemaker"; and to the Church of the Saviour in Washington, D.C. (with its remarkable shepherd, Gordon Cosby), which understood, comforted and steadied me on a path that reaffirmed those concepts. These positive people more than offset the unpleasant encounters with those who use the label *peacenik* to describe people who have a sincere yearning to follow the church's teaching.

At home my brother and I had learned (wrongly) as children to avoid conflict at any price. That too shaped our lives. So nothing has ever made me happier than that moment when he came flying to the Middle East in spite of his fear, believed the strange things I told him and gave over his whole life to helping me. "Brother's" value as a teacher of law, theology, ethics and psychology is a resource of immeasurable content to a needy society.

Elizabeth Aldridge took the tear-stained yellow sheets of scribbling and added her own tears to her skilled word processing. Otherwise there would have been no diary from which to make a book. As other families entered the small circle after I broke the silence, we supported and taught each other. Especially precious to me is Elaine Collett, who became "the most forgotten," perhaps, because although she is American, her hostage husband, Alec, is British and they are further destined to a confusing identification status because she is black and Alec is white. Elaine's courage is stunning, and she inspires everyone who meets her. I promised Elaine as well as Eric Jacobson (son of hostage David Jacobson) that I would tell "our story" somehow. But I've known all along that there is almost no way that I can thank them and all of the other people—Jews, Muslims and Christians . . . Arabs, Israelis, Syrians, Palestinians, Lebanese, British, Americans—who, as did my brother, listened and knew it was true and wanted the story to make a difference for peace. Many of them are in the text; all of them are in the unedited diary; and they will be a part of my life and love as long as I live. And, God willing *(inshallah)*, other books will continue the story.

A brilliant teacher, Eric Zencey of Goddard College, led me into an understanding of how my story fits into the History of Peacemaking and enriched my life far beyond what is indicated by my master's degree. Another professor very much like him at Columbia Teachers College. Bill Sayres, is guiding me toward a doctorate in peace studies. It is thrilling to be allowed the privilege to learn like this. A Yale student interning with the National Council on U.S.-Arab Relations, Paula Jacobsen, who is my colleague and "adopted daughter," edited, typed and researched the early drafts of this book, all the while enriching our lives with her gentle presence.

In my seemingly endless college career, InterVarsity has been my favorite life-enrichment colloquium, a place to think and talk out loud about things that really matter, without fear of ridicule. InterVarsity staff David and Nancy Moore have helped thousands of young people through the transitional, troubling years into stable, happy lives. It was David who saw my diary as a book and called InterVarsity Press. Lynda Stephenson is the editor who, working with my patient, generous husband, made my diary-thesis into the kind of "real writing" that is called a book, and I am grateful to them both.

Lastly, Frank Wade and the vestry at St. Alban's Episcopal Church in Washington, D.C., along with Michelle Jourdak and Jack Dunfey of the Human Rights Project and Ellsworth Culver of Mercy Corps International, helped sustain me financially when I was running out of money with which to travel, study and write. They opened not only their pocketbooks, offices and homes; they opened their hearts when I was sure mine was going to break.

Jerry and Ells and Landrum Bolling have recently taken some of these new friends to the Middle East for their first visit, and all our expectations are high for enlarging the circle of concern and dedication to reconciliation and peace in this problem—*our* problem, because we *are* involved.

14

"Journalist Missing in Beirut."

Washington Post, March 8, 1984

DECEMBER 1983

THE CAMERA IS ROLLING. The dark, mustached man in a sweater and jacket, microphone in hand, leans forward from his crouched position near a broken wall. Behind him, a block away in some badly damaged buildings, crouch militia men. They are firing below into an army caravan. Cars behind the army caravan are stranded. People are taking cover.

The man begins to speak into the camera loudly, to be heard over the sporadic gunfire and sirens.

"Lebanese soldiers rolled into a Shiite Muslim Amal Movement trap by the Iranian Embassy, and the CNN crew is trapped right along with them." Gunfire interrupts him. Soldiers in the background are moving in and out of sight. The camera continues to roll, and the minutes pass. Finally, the firing stops as the caravan, as well as the rest of the cars, begins to move away slowly.

The man waits a few seconds, watches cautiously, then turns to the camera again:

"Within ten minutes, the skirmish was over. The troops moved down the road, and the traffic began to roll again.
—JERRY LEVIN, CNN, BEIRUT."

JANUARY 22, 1984

BEIRUT

Sitting in my window seat on the plane, I craned my neck to see the city below. I couldn't sit still, I was so excited. I hadn't seen my husband, Jerry, since December, when he'd come ahead alone to begin work as Cable News Network's Beirut Bureau Chief.

He'd written wonderful things: "The people of Beirut are almost irresistible in their spunkiness and dogged persever-ance."

And scary things: "There is no night life. Curfew is at 8 p.m. We never go anywhere without a driver. But during the day, walking seems okay. There is no longer the swimming in the morning and skiing in the afternoon you've read about."

I listened to the wonderful things and ignored the scary ones, because one of the last things he'd written to me was about our "adventure together."

"You'll have stories to tell the grandchildren for the rest of your days," he'd promised. And that's what I was thinking as we touched down. Beirut was safe enough for Americans at that point. The U.S. Marines were guarding the airport. But in a peace-keeping capacity, I was told. And it looked so beautiful from the air, nestled between the blue of the Mediterranean and the snows of Mount Lebanon. Like a jewel on the edge of the sea. "The Paris of the Middle East," it was once called.

Finally we landed. After being herded through customs, I collected my luggage and passed armed guards at several checkpoints inside the airport. Finally I made my way outside. They were moving us through to an outer courtyard.

That's where I saw Jerry, leaning on a barricade. After giving me a long hug, he introduced his Lebanese driver, Fahd, a short, wiry man with a mustache and slicked-back hair. "I will keep Jerry safe! I will not let him out from under my armpit!" Fahd declared. "Jerry is my brother! By day, by night, by God, I will watch out after him!"

I stared warmly at my Jewish husband, his dark eyes twinkling as he grinned at his driver. I loved seeing the broadjawed, mustached face I'd missed so much. And then as I looked around us, I couldn't help noticing something. "Jerry, you certainly blend in well here—" I said, glancing around at all the dark-eyed, dark-haired Lebanese milling around us.

"Well, we're all Semites," Jerry laughed, grabbing my arm. "C'mon, let's go home."

We rode away in Fahd's dusty Mercedes. And that drive was my first clue that this was going to be quite a different experience than what I'd envisioned. Hanging from his rearview mirror was a plastic picture of the Ayatollah Khomeini. That was shock enough, but Fahd's driving, much of which was at top speed and often on the sidewalks, made me dig my nails into the seat. I kept thinking of a bumper sticker I'd laughed about back in Washington: "If you don't like my driving, keep off the sidewalks." I wasn't laughing now.

There was nothing defensive about driving on Beirut streets, I quickly learned. One could get caught literally all day in traffic jams, due to the sporadic fighting at the traffic lights which hadn't worked for years, a real problem for a newsman and his crew. Fahd's remedy—drive aggressively wherever and however the situation called for.

We turned, and the traffic thinned out. Fahd was back on the streets again, so I began looking around. The jewel I had seen from the air, on closer inspection, was scarred, ruined. The land was pockmarked. Buildings were shattered. "Why?" I couldn't help thinking.

" 'Paris of the Middle East,' " I mumbled. "Isn't that what people called Beirut?"

Fahd answered, over his shoulder, "No more." He swerved around some rubble in the street. "Someday again. *Inshallah*—God willing."

I smiled and nodded, squeezing Jerry's hand. "Maybe while I'm here I'll become an expert on the Middle East."

"You don't have time left," Fahd grunted and swerved onto another street. I was afraid to ask what he meant.

As we careened down the roads, I gaped at the devastation outside my window. It was overwhelming. "Picture World War 2 movies," Jerry had written. It was the right image. Nothing seemed untouched. A few minutes later, though, we passed a building which looked totally out of place. It looked new, painted and clean. "Smith's Supermarket," the sign proudly announced.

"It's been destroyed by shells three times, and Smith keeps rebuilding fancier than the last," Jerry said.

I noticed another incongruity. Amid all the battered buildings, there were beauty parlors—every block or so, women with perfectly coiffed hair came and went from them. And almost all of the parlors had advertisements in their windows boasting, "We have a generator." I looked at Jerry, puzzled.

Jerry smiled. "The electricity is only on during certain hours, and often not then."

We pulled up to the apartment building. Home was going to be an apartment in a building on the edge of a high bluff by the sea. It had been rented by CNN for the bureau chief Jerry replaced. Jerry and Fahd lugged my steamer trunk onto the elevator. Fahd hit the button and grinned. The electricity was working.

In a moment, we were inside the apartment on the sixth floor. Fahd looked the apartment over with an approving glance and then, still grinning, backed out through the double steel doors, clanging them ceremoniously. He had come in earlier and left flowers and iced champagne.

The apartment itself was lovely, with a bedroom that opened onto a balcony overlooking the Mediterranean Sea. I walked out onto the balcony and breathed deeply. Below, I could see a soccer field, and running along the Mediterranean shore was the seaside boulevard called the Corniche. The water was blue and sparkling against the white sea wall. Gorgeous . . . yet, there—parked in the middle of the perfect view—was a battleship.

"What in the world is a battleship doing out there?" I asked.

"That's the *New Jersey*," Jerry answered, walking out on the balcony with me.

"An American battleship?"

Jerry nodded. "It's there to keep the peace is how the Administration explains it. I wish it weren't there. Many Lebanese don't see us as peace keepers, and it puts all Americans in a compromising position."

Then, I looked closer at the soccer field below. There were deep ruts crisscrossing it, the kind made unmistakably by military equipment. I was to find out that they were made by mobile guns rolled in during the night and aimed over our apartment at the hills encircling our city.

Here I was, a conservative, Southern Christian woman who would follow her liberal, Yankee Jewish husband any-where, even to this predominately Muslim world very few Westerners understood or even gave much thought.

And there were guns outside my window.

Years ago, Jerry and I had made a pact to go if he were ever offered an overseas assignment, and when that assign-ment was Beirut, we didn't hesitate. Beirut was "where the action was," as newsmen love to say. And this husband of mine was a newsman through and through, the kind that believes in truth above everything. In the ten years of our relationship, Jerry has refused to lie about anything. He looks me, or anyone, in the eye and tells it straight, no matter how uncomfortable the telling. So I am sure he made the danger clear to me.

But whatever he'd told me, when Jerry came home to our Chicago apartment on an icy December day to say he had been asked to go to Beirut, my excitement overrode my fear. Jerry told me he was to go in as acting bureau chief to help straighten out editorial, administrative and financial prob-lems, as well as to be a correspondent. I was aware of Leb-anon's years of civil war. I'd read of the 1982 invasion of Lebanon by Israel, and the controversy swirling around the country. So we had only ourselves to blame for being in the middle of Lebanon's war, if anything should go wrong.

But nothing could have prepared us for what would happen to us within the next year. In three months, our lives would be turned inside out.

For now, though, I was back with this man who made me feel young and loved again when I thought I'd missed my last chance at both. That was what was important to me, what was real to me. Not the *New Jersey* or the guns outside. Being with Jerry, that was real. Love is far more than blind at times. In those short weeks apart, I'd missed him in a way that even surprised me. I told myself I did not want to be apart again, for any reason—ever.

And that night, lying there in our bedroom with the warm, lazy sea breeze blowing in on us, I held him as if I'd never let him get away again.

FEBRUARY 1, 1984

BEIRUT

During the next several weeks, I began to meet the Beirut people Jerry had described—attractive, spunky, doggedly persistent. I set out to learn all I could about the city, its people and its culture, and about what was happening around me. I was embarrassed to admit that until recently I would have been hard pressed to pinpoint the exact location of Lebanon on a map of the Middle East and that I found the reasons for the Lebanese conflict baffling.

The people, though, *were* fascinating. Walking down the streets were well-dressed women fresh from those beauty parlors, stepping over the debris from shelling the night before. The contrast was almost absurd. As I began to meet people, I would receive formal invitations in true Middle East fashion that would say that the hostess would be "at home" on a certain afternoon for guests "if the situation permits."

My landlord was Mr. Ghannoum, who wore a flowing

abaya, the traditional, colorful Arabic robe. He had several children, and I spent quite a bit of time with them, especially his beautiful seventeen-year-old daughter, Hana. Also in my building lived a man named Ed Kellermeyer, an American businessman who'd spent years in Lebanon working in commodities. They would all teach me many things in the weeks to come and become my lifelong friends.

I quickly located the Arabic Episcopal Church. I'd always made my first friends at church wherever I'd lived. There, on my first Sunday in Beirut, I met Violet Copti, a Palestinian married to an Egyptian. They were both teachers, her husband a professor at the International School. Violet was the one who taught me how to get around in the streets, in spite of her obvious embarrassment over the piles of rotting garbage and broken concrete. As we got to know each other, she told me about their past, but only a small part. Even though they were highly educated, they were caught here in Beirut with no place to go. Their real home was in Jerusalem. But one day while they were away, an Israeli family had simply moved in, so the Coptis lost their home. That was all I could ever learn of the story because whenever I mentioned it her eyes would well up with tears so quickly that I didn't have the heart to ask more. "God is our refuge," she would tell me, forcing a smile. "We have been more fortunate than most."

Violet told me of a tiny British church, All Souls of Beirut, which was meeting in the German Embassy Chapel because its own building had been destroyed by rocket shells. The rector, Peter Crooks, served as chaplain to the British Embassy and was director for Inter-Varsity Fellowship a group which I had worked with since college days. Peter, his wife, Nancy, and their five-year-old son, Timmy, became instant friends of mine too. And Peter introduced me to three missionaries: Joan, a Briton; Brenda, a South African; and Vicki, an Australian. They were amazing, so full of life, so deter-mined to help, moving supplies back and forth to areas that needed them, finding needs and trying to fill them. I was fascinated.

Our church group was so small we often held our Eucha-rist services and Bible studies in our homes. And as we met, we could hear shelling off in the distance. But being together calmed us.

One time, as we sipped tea in my flat, I asked this young priest, "Are you frightened, Peter?"

"Yes," he answered. "When I'm walking home at night and there's shooting," he said quietly, "I try to whistle or sing, or I work my prayers into the tune." It was not unusual in those first few weeks for my new friends to come to our home for dinner and be forced to spend the night because they dared not travel after curfew.

While Jerry and his cameras worked to broadcast "truth" back to the States, I realized, as I grew close to these excep-tional people in such a short time, that I was learning a lot about "truth" myself. I had been looking for what I hoped would be the ultimate "truth" for years, patching together credits in theological studies wherever I followed Jerry. It felt strange, but here in Beirut, among these compassionate mis-sionaries who seemed so devout yet were so normal and funny and real, I sensed I would learn more than in my frantic studies in Birmingham, Houston, Washington and Chicago divinity schools. The politics here were so confus-ing. The people were not.

I'll never forget one night when Peter, Nancy and little Timmy were with me, and we were deep in a discussion about the fighting when Timmy suddenly asked, "Daddy, who are the goodies, and who are the baddies?"

I listened closely as Peter tried to answer that one. He

paused. I still remember his answer: "The goodies . . . are the people who talk instead of shoot, Timmy."

I was just beginning to learn how complex the problems were over here, struggling to understand all the tribes and sects and reasons each one had for the war we were caught in. Often, I wanted to ask the same question myself. During the little free time we had together those first few weeks, Jerry and I would lie in bed and gaze out at the moonlight over the battleship *New Jersey* outside our window, and I would bombard him with questions, trying to grasp it all.

"Sis," Jerry began, "there are four major sects here, the Shiite Muslims, the Sunni Muslims, the Druze and the Maronite Christians."

"Our landlord, Mr. Ghannoum, is a Muslim," I added.

"Yes, he is, but he is a Sunni Muslim. In Lebanon, they're more upper-class and liberal than the Shiites. The Shiites are generally poorer, less well educated and religiously more fundamental. They are Iranian-style Muslims who look to the Ayatollah as their spiritual leader."

"The fighting—it's about the government?" I asked.

"Right," Jerry said. "Although Lebanon is a democracy, it's not organized the way ours is. There was an unusual verbal agreement, the National Pact, made about forty years ago when the government was established. Since the Christians were the majority then, and the Maronites were the most powerful Christian sect, the agreement was that the president of Lebanon would always be a Maronite Christian and that the Maronites would always run the army."

"Always?"

"Always," Jerry nodded. "But the prime minister would always be Sunni and the speaker of the parliament would always be Shiite. Forty years ago the population was probably fifty-five per cent Christian to forty-five per cent Muslim and

Druze. Now that proportion is probably reversed."

"East Beirut is still mostly Christian, isn't it?" I interrupted.

"Yes. But West Beirut—that's another thing. More Muslims live in West Beirut now than Christians. There hasn't been a census since the early 1930s, but no one disputes the Shiite Muslims when they claim they're underrepresented here. They want the agreement changed, and the Maronites don't. The Muslims, especially the Shiites, want a bigger piece of the pie. That's what the civil war is about—and that's why the Green Line is there."

The Green Line. It divides mostly Muslim-and-Druze West Beirut from Christian East Beirut, and it seemed so odd to me. Violet's children could not go to school, I remembered, because their school was on the other side of this line.

Just the day before, Jerry asked another of his drivers to take us down to the Green Line. The driver was Salim. He was a kind, gentle, grandfatherly Lebanese who drove with his head, calculating the best ways to go through the chaos, compared to Fahd's seat-of-the-pants method. And as we drove close, I could see that all the streets cutting across the Green Line were blocked off or heavily barricaded. Jerry told me that when the fighting flairs up, the handful of official crossings across the line are closed. You could be caught on one side or the other, and you could also be shot trying to cross. It was like a battle line, like the one between South Korea and North Korea, or East and West Berlin. And that day, Jerry had urged me to get out and walk near it with him to get a feeling of what it was like to be at the center of the danger zone.

"Salim says he is a Druze. Who are they?" I went on, feeling safe and warm there in our bedroom, leaning toward Jerry.

"They're an offshoot of Islam, sort of a mystery sect because their rituals are secret. They've been in the mountains for years and years. They're a significant force," Jerry answered.

"And the Hizballah?"

"An extremist Shiite organization supported by money, arms and also personnel from Iran. They've been known to use terrorism. *Hizballah* means 'Party of God.' They've got a militia. It's pretty secret too," Jerry explained. "They want to install a government like Iran's. Run by religious leaders. But they're not the biggest Shiite political faction. That's Amal. The word means 'hope' because even though they don't want a revolution like the Hizballah, they do want to restructure the present government. Syria backs Amal. They've got a big militia. So do the Druze. And Syria backs them too."

"Does *everybody* have a militia?" I said, already knowing the answer. It sounded like warlords battling for control of territories. I had even been told by others that some Shiites were working both sides of the street. They'll work for Amal during the day and Hizballah at night.

"What about the invasion by Israel in 1982?" I prodded, trying to get it all straight.

"Well, the Maronite Christians and their militia, called the Phalange, thought Israel would help them keep the Muslims and Druze in their place, so they cooperated with the invasion," Jerry explained. "Then the Phalange . . . got out of hand."

I knew we were both thinking about the massacre of Sabra and Shatilla. Some people wrote that it rivaled the Holocaust in its ferocity—the Phalange slaughtering women and children in the Palestinian refugee camps while unprotesting Israeli guards stood by. The fact was hard for me to comprehend, and I didn't want to at that moment. The wind suddenly seemed to chill. I got up and closed the draperies over the window, so I could not see the battleship in the sea below.

One day, I asked Fahd to take me to see Sabra and Shatilla. Even though it was a quiet day, I could feel his reluctance to show me the depressing, ruined camps. As we drove up, all I could see was rubble, tin, ruined buildings, dust and garbage—and children playing nearby. We got out of the car and stood beside it, neither of us wanting to venture into the area. He watched me a moment, to see how I was reacting; then he spat out the story.

"Phalange—" he muttered, as if the word were poison. "They came in and shot the children. They ripped open the bellies of pregnant women and killed the unborn. After dark, the Israelis lit torches so the Phalange could see better to kill."

I thought of the accounts I'd read. When the Israelis invaded Lebanon, it was to knock out Palestinian control in the South. Everyone believed the Israelis when they said that's where the invasion would end. Instead, as Fahd explained, "they swept up into Beirut, through refugee camps, killing Palestinian women, men, children . . . Muslim and Christian."

Ellen Siegel, an American Jewish nurse whom I came to know later, had been working in the Sabra camp at the time and was caught in the massacre. She told of the high explosives, the machine-gun fire, the Israeli flares lighting up the night and the absolute helplessness of the refugee-camp residents as they flooded into the hospital and then abandoned it when explosives hit nearby, cracking windows, pouring in smoke. Only the critically ill and the staff had stayed behind. At first, they even threatened to kill her and the other workers. But finally the army escorted them out, and she told how she walked by scores of dead bodies and watched an Israeli bulldozer covering a mass grave.

Meanwhile, across the border to the South, hundreds of thousands of Israelis poured into their streets in protest, demanding an official inquiry. What I painfully remember was one front-page picture of bloated corpses heaped on top of one another in a narrow alleyway. I felt my stomach surge.

"Christians are *murderers,*" Fahd growled.

I winced. I couldn't *stand* hearing the word *Christian,* a word that meant so much to me, being used in such a context. "They weren't Christians," I said quietly.

Fahd didn't understand. I was to learn that here in the Middle East, a whole new terminology was needed to separate religion and politics from personal faith. It had come to the point that everyone was forced to redefine their terms because the old ones held such negative meaning. Even before Sabra and Shatilla, to many Lebanese the term *Christian* automatically meant "murderer." Just as in the months ahead, *Shiite Muslim* would come to mean "terrorist." The language of true faith had to find other labels. *True Believer* became the term my friends and I used when talking about our faith.

"Fahd, how did it all come to this?" I said wearily, leaning against his car.

Fahd shrugged angrily. "There was time when Christians, Muslims and Jews all lived together here in peace."

"What happened?"

Fahd shrugged again. "Maybe people got too fat, too rich. People from outside, they came in, things changed. And Palestinians, they came spilling out of Israel, pushed out of their land. Some people in Lebanon, maybe they felt threatened.

"*Jihad,*" he mumbled, picking up a pebble and rolling it around in his hands as he gazed across the ruined landscape.

"What?" I said.

"*Jihad*—it means 'standing against oppression . . . defending oneself.' Jihad is the whole way of life for us Shiites. The Hizballah says they are the warriors in a holy war. They see only that Lebanon should be Shiite Muslim. As a matter of fact they also refer to themselves as Islamic Jihad. Christian murderers should not be in power, they say."

I winced once again at the juxtaposition of those two words.

"We must go," he finally said. I was ready.

That night, back at our apartment, I told Jerry of my trip. "None of it makes sense, Jerry. Why didn't the Israelis around the camps stop the Phalange instead of helping them? What is the Israeli government going to do about it?" I went on and on. Jerry is the grandson of a widely respected turn-of-the-century rabbi, and when we'd married, I'd taken the Jewish cause to heart. Now, though, I felt a sensory overload with all these conflicting situations and emotions. "Of all people! Didn't the Israeli army know there would be a violent retaliation someday? Did they really think that these people would not question the murdering of so many Arabs?"

Jerry quietly answered. "Have you ever known of a country, anywhere, including the U.S., that tried itself for its own mistakes?"

I studied his face. "What do you mean?"

"I mean simply that all of Israel was torn apart by this incident. There was an official investigation and much public agonizing."

"So, what did they do to compensate the victims?"

He stared at me with sad, tired eyes, and I let it go, because I knew there was no answer. We didn't say anything for a moment or two.

"*Phalange,*" I said, finally, "it doesn't truly mean 'Christian,' so maybe *Israeli* doesn't necessarily mean 'Jew.' "

"Not in the best sense anymore."

"Maybe not—yet," Jerry finally sighed. "Maybe that will come when they . . . we . . . are not so frightened about survival."

But I kept thinking about what Salim, the kind, grandfatherly driver, had said one day. We'd been talking about the Palestinians, and he'd been his quiet self, until suddenly he remarked, "Couldn't the Jews give them just a little place to live?"

Work for Jerry meant fourteen-hour days and often longer. His offices were in the Commodore Hotel annex only about a fifteen-minute walk from our apartment. Many of the foreign news bureaus were headquartered there. Our day would start at 6:00 A.M. I'd get up to fix him breakfast, to be with him a few minutes, because I wouldn't see him again until late that night. So I tried to settle into my own routine.

I signed up for classes at the Near East School of Theology and made plans to take Arabic lessons at Beirut University College. The rest of my day I began filling with Beirut. On the way home one day, I noticed a battered but still sturdy building with a sign that said, "Cultural Center."

There was a young boy outside sweeping up glass from the shelling the night before. I said, "Pardon me, but I used to do quite a bit of work with art councils back in the States. Maybe I could help here. Is there someone I could talk to about that?"

The boy brightened and told me to follow him into the building. Inside was his father, Mr. Sami Salibi, the founder of the Cultural Center of West Beirut, a school where this one man stubbornly continued to teach Beirut's children to sing, play piano and paint, all through the fighting.

34

I found the slight, older man with tears in his eyes. One of their dorms had caught fire during the shelling the night before, and several of his students had been missing for a while. They had just found them safe and sound. They'd escaped by shinnying down the drainpipes. But Mr. Salibi was still not over it.

After our introductions, he explained his dream. "When this war is ended," he sighed, "I want these children to have their culture." He told me of the emotional wounds that war can make on children, and how he believed strongly in the therapeutic capacity of music. I had always been fascinated by the concept too and had studied a bit about it. So I told him about my background as an arts administrator in the States, how I felt all the arts communicated on a different level to people's needs, and before I knew it, we were spending long hours planning for the future of his remarkable school.

Often, we would walk through the battered building. We'd move around the sandbags lying around the entrance and step over the window-glass remnants, and I'd try not to stare at the blood spattered here and there. Inside, though, there were children working and playing everywhere. There were art rooms and music rooms, and before the worst shelling ruined it, there was even a dance floor.

The visit to the school I remember most was the time we passed a room where a group of children, eight or nine years old, were happily singing.

"What are they singing?" I asked Mr. Salibi.

"Arabic folk songs," he said with pride.

My eyes gravitated to one child in particular there in the front row. Her high, sweet voice was rising above the other voices, as she cocked her head happily to the side. She was smaller than the others, much smaller, with long curly black

35

hair and dark eyes that seem to be gazing off in the distance, with a somewhat pixieish expression on her face.

"Who is that little girl?" I asked, pointing.

"Ginwa? She is blind," Mr. Salibi answered.

We could hear the Arabic folk song throughout the rest of our walk through the building, and it stayed in my mind long afterwards. And so did little Ginwa. She was the one I pictured as we made our plans for music-therapy programs and for aid for the Cultural Center.

On one of our days together, I noticed that the pen Mr. Salibi always carried in his pocket had been replaced with a toothbrush. Mr. Salibi saw me looking, and with an embarrassed smile, he pulled it out and turned it over. The other end of the toothbrush was a pen. "For emergencies," he said. He had fashioned the invention for his Beirut lifestyle, in case he ever got caught after curfew in the wrong part of town. In a sweet serendipity, Mr. Salibi was a beekeeper. In the midst of his city's war, he kept beehives and, although he often sold the honey to make money for his school, usually he simply gave it to the children for their nourishment. And many times, while delivering honey, he told me he'd be unable to get through checkpoints, so he would be forced to stay where he was overnight. Hence the toothbrush/pen.

As I explored my area of the city cautiously, I noticed there were checkpoints everywhere. Soldiers or militiamen would appear from nowhere with their guns in hand, and shelling could be heard off and on all through the day—all of these scary things were a way of life for these people, and they adapted.

Yet the city could be so beautiful at times too. Sometimes I felt I was living in a dream that turned into a nightmare and then back into a dream, over and over.

For instance, there is a street in Beirut that was once comparable to the Champs Elysée in Paris, with its sidewalk cafes and social life, and even its French-influenced architecture. The street is called the Hamra, and strolling down it was like entering a fantasy. The Beirut residents hated to let the image go so much that here, in the middle of war, they did all they could to keep the feeling alive along this one street, with its waiters in tuxedos and its elegant cabaret atmosphere.

One time during those first few weeks, Jerry was able to get away from work to have lunch with me, so we met at one of those open-air restaurants. We were sitting at a table close to the street at the Cafe Modca, enjoying the sunshine and being with each other, when one of Jerry's news crews spotted us and began filming us. Everything seemed so wonderful at that moment, I looked at the camera and flippantly said, "War? What war?" I'll never forget Jerry's stinging response.

"Don't *ever* say that," he said in a flat, even voice.

A few days later we experienced the siege of West Beirut, and I was never again to forget that I was in the middle of a war.

FEBRUARY 6, 1984

BEIRUT

The day started normally. I was on my way back to our apartment from visiting a new friend who had just had a baby. I'd been working most of the morning on plans to help the Cultural Center, and I was feeling so good about finding my niche in this new world that I was actually singing as I walked into my apartment. Until the rocket shot past my window.

The front of my apartment was mostly glass, so I saw the path of it, from left to right. I froze. I couldn't connect what I saw with reality.

Almost immediately, I heard my upstairs neighbor, Ed Kellermeyer, the American businessman, at my door commanding me to follow him.

"Can I get my Bible?" I asked.

"No! NOW! NOW!" he was yelling.

I grabbed my Bible on the way out anyway, my knees

shaking, and ran down the steps to my landlord's apartment where we all would spend the terrifying afternoon and night together. It was the beginning of the siege of West Beirut. The Amal and Druze militias were battling the army for control of this side of the Green Line. West Beirut.

Mr. Ghannoum's children, a girl of four and a boy of two, whimpered softly each time a shell exploded near us. Hana, the older daughter, was also there, looking brave. Mr. Ghannoum spread his abaya on the polished stone floor of his first-story apartment, and he gathered the two into his arms to comfort them. I kept picturing guns on the soccer field pointed over the top of our apartment building at the mountains above.

At the next explosion, Ed said he had counted seventeen direct hits nearby. "This is the worst ever!" he scowled. "Even worse than Israel's bombardment in '82." He handed me a cup of tea from a tray offered by one of the servant girls employed by the Ghannoums. They looked so calm. I tried to drink the tea, but I was finding it very hard to swallow.

The crash of exploding shells was deafening, and the electricity flickered off and on, often leaving us in the yellow half-light of the evening sun, the only light that filtered through the heavily curtained windows.

"Why? Why is this happening?" I kept saying. It was the single incessant question in my mind and on my lips since I had arrived. I put my head between my knees and braced for the next explosion.

"Courage, Sis!" shouted Mr. Ghannoum, smiling broadly at me. I noticed for the first time a picture of President Reagan on the wall above him.

"I can tell you why, but you won't like it," Ed answered me, wiping the perspiration from his balding head. Another hit exploded nearby. "Thirty-two!" he counted, then said, "The

Shiite and Druze are demonstrating their rage, Sis, at the government, especially at President Amin Gemayel, the leader of the minority Christian-dominated government we have been supporting with our ships and Marines."

" 'We?' "

"The U.S. It's like Vietnam, in my mind," he said. "You'd think we would learn not to meddle in other people's civil wars, especially ones we know we can't win," he added, pulling out a pastel-colored Turkish cigarette and lighting it.

"I thought we were peace keepers," I said.

"That's what you were supposed to think, you and the rest of the American voters who probably don't know where to find Lebanon on a map," he snorted.

I winced at the truth of that.

"You want a run-down of what's been going on lately?" he asked.

"Yes," I said, and I took another cup of tea, tried to curl up as best I could on Mr. Ghannoum's mounds of pillows and listened.

"In October, a suicide bomber wiped out the U.S. Marine barracks at Beirut International Airport. Remember? That killed 241. In December, a truck loaded with explosives rammed the U.S. Embassy in Kuwait. Iran-backed Shiite Muslims were behind both incidents."

"But I don't understand. They're mad at us? How are we 'butting in'? "

"Last September—that's when Reagan's special envoy Robert McFarlane urged the President to allow the U.S. naval forces in the Mediterranean to end our neutrality, take sides and start shooting into the mountains, against Shiite, Druze and Syrian positions. When we did that we stopped being neutral peace keepers, and came down with a bang on the side of the minority Christian-dominated government. It

41

really sparked trouble."

As I listened to the shells and to Ed, this whole idea of the Muslims' and Druze's retaliation against American targets was, to my way of thinking, still something that happened to someone else. And when it did, the only way it would touch us was that Jerry would broadcast the stories back home. We weren't the military. Things would be all right for us.

I could hear Ed grumbling. "It didn't just start here, you know. Israelis and Palestinians—they keep killing each other over that same piece of land. Many of the problems all over the Middle East stem from it. Especially the Palestinians being kicked out of their land by the Israelis. First, in '48, and then after the Six Day War in '67. . . . No place to go, spilling over into other Arab countries who don't know what to do with them either. So what do they do? They start fighting with each other. People are just getting desperate. Everywhere." It was quiet a moment, then we heard another shell. "Thirty-three," Ed said automatically.

In the eerie light, I saw my landlord and his little children entwined in a heap on the pillows. They had fallen asleep. Then, a moment later, when all was quiet again, Mr. Ghannoum got up and took down the picture of President Reagan.

Through the night, we listened on the radio to the BBC. The Red Cross building downtown was on fire, it reported. We could see through the cracks of our curtains that neighboring houses were on fire. More than one hundred had already been killed and three hundred wounded, but the ambulances couldn't get to the wounded because Amal had announced that they would shoot anyone on the street.

As the hours passed, I couldn't stop thinking about Jerry caught at the Bureau about a mile away. Between us, there were several blocks likely to be impassable because of the curfew, and I was feeling sick with anxiety and worry over him. So about 2 A.M., Mr. Ghannoum led me into Hana's bedroom, where he managed miraculously to get a line through to Jerry at the CNN offices at the Commodore Hotel.

"She loves you too much!" he told Jerry before handing me the phone. Then, after we consoled each other with the fact that both of us were for the moment safe and fairly sound, Jerry laid the phone on his desk and left it there for the rest of the night so I could feel connected to him as I listened to the sounds coming from the newsroom. He told me later that Fahd and he were the only ones there because he had sent everyone to safety in the hotel's basement. Fahd stayed because he had refused to leave Jerry alone. I could hear shells exploding outside his office. And I could hear him give a live interview by phone to CNN's news desk in the USA. He was speaking from under his desk.

All night long, I sat there on the floor, with the phone pressed to my ear, listening to the sounds of Jerry's newsroom. That phone call was a present from Mr. Ghannoum. And I would never forget it.

Morning came at last, and the militias had won. They had taken control of West Beirut. Amal's leader, Nabih Berri, a name I was to become quite familiar with, now controlled West Beirut. The siege was over.

When we were convinced the worst of the fighting and shelling had stopped, we cautiously moved toward the window. The sun was up.

Through the morning, we could still hear what seemed like futile bursts of gunfire. Jerry sent Fahd to the apartment to pick me up and drive me through the new Shiite checkpoints to Jerry's offices at the hotel.

"Don't be afraid, Sis," Fahd said proudly, "I am the best driver in Beirut. I will get you there safely." And he did.

Jerry booked me a room in the hotel until the last of the

fighting had finished so we would not be apart. During the day, I sat on a sofa at the Bureau and quietly watched him work. The newsroom was hectic as the reporters were logging story after story about what was happening to Lebanon.

After a few days, even the occasional bursts of fire had ceased, so Jerry and I returned to our apartment, Jerry going to work, with Fahd driving him from doorstep to doorstep between the Bureau and home. I kept the radio tuned to the BBC for reports on the hour, like a prayer vigil. The war in Lebanon was the lead story every day. The British commentators spoke of America's "diplomatic failure" in the Middle East.

I soon found that my Arabic class had been disbanded because most of the students had fled. Since Beirut University College, like all schools in Beirut, was closed "until the situation permits," I made arrangements to have private lessons.

Nabih Berri announced from his heavily guarded headquarters that he would soon have the city running again and ordered his militia to be peaceful. We were all worried, but the journalists seemed to like Nabih Berri, and so did many of the Lebanese, and not just Muslims. I remember after the siege, Shiite refugees from the fighting swarmed in and occupied the School for the Blind, which had long been run by a dedicated group of Christian missionaries. So the students and the missionaries went to Berri and asked him to give the school back to them. Berri ordered his troops to move the refugees out and give the school back to the missionaries. It seemed that many people I talked to thought Berri should have a chance at bringing order from the chaos.

Still, most Americans were frightened. Many had fled Beirut. Yet the journalists felt relatively safe because their work was essentially respected by all sides. There always seemed to be more reporters arriving.

And then within a very short time, President Reagan announced the withdrawal of the Marines. My seventy-five-year-old mother telexed us from Birmingham: "Can Sis come out with the Marines?" We had smiled at each other and ignored it. The press was safe—safe enough, we assured ourselves.

Jerry covered the Marines' departure. I met him on the beach minutes after the Marines had been withdrawn to awaiting ships. Salim was driving us along the Corniche, the crescent road that hugged the Mediterranean. We had grown accustomed to the sight of the U.S.S. *New Jersey* cruising offshore. I was absently gazing at it and the blue-green sea around it, when suddenly the *New Jersey* was firing big, round, loud salvos. It was the first time I had ever seen a battleship fire. And it looked like it was firing straight at us!

"What are they doing! Are they trying to kill us?" I screamed.

"No, it's over our heads," Jerry said, calmly. "They're firing way over our heads into the hills. That's their parting shot."

MARCH 7, 8:15 A.M.

BEIRUT

AFTER CHECKING THE LOCK *on the iron security door of their apartment, Jerry Levin rushes out of the apartment building. He is later than normal. Sis has already left. He walks briskly through various streets, up Rue California, to Rue Bliss, on his way to the CNN offices at the hotel.*

But as he nears the Saudi Embassy, Jerry feels a tap on his shoulder, and a voice, in a thick accent, says softly, "Excuse me."

Jerry turns. The man pushes a small, green handgun into his stomach. Then he clasps his hand on Jerry's shoulder and hisses, "You come."

A small car pulls up, the back door flies open, and the man pushes Jerry inside, roughly shoving his head into the seat.

"Close eyes! Close eyes! You see, I kill!" the man screams, as the car roars away.

MARCH 7, 1984

BEIRUT

It was Ash Wednesday, a day of penitence in the Episcopal Church, the first day of the Holy Season leading up to Easter. So that the men could come, Peter had scheduled church services that night, and I was looking forward to it, hoping I could get my nonbelieving husband to join me. It was a beautiful day. I had just finished my theology class at the Near East School of Theology, and I was on my way to Violet's home, climbing up the hill to Madame Curie Street. Violet was giving me Arabic lessons at her home. I always had to pay close attention to where I was going because all the signs were in that complicated language. The Arabic letters still looked confusingly alike to me. Violet and her family lived in a flat five floors up. The "electric," as they called it, was out, so I had to walk up the five flights.

The children were always home since they could not cross the Green Line to get to school. They waited for me at the landing with a tiny candle, and they hid behind the sofa and giggled at my efforts to repeat the sounds Violet asked me to make.

"Would you like to share our lunch with us?" Violet asked.

"No, thanks," I smiled. "Jerry is going to try hard to take me to the Hamra."

I had left Jerry back in the apartment when I'd gone off to class several hours before. I felt strange leaving the apartment with him still there. Usually he was up and gone before 6:00 A.M. But for the first time since I'd been there, the situation had quieted down enough to allow him to sleep later than usual. I'd left him shaving at the bathroom mirror. I'd kissed him good-by, then wiped the foam from my lips and hurried toward the door.

"Could you possibly take off for lunch?" I called back.

He knew it was a Christian holiday, a special time for me. Jerry considered himself an atheist. I thought of him as an intellectual agnostic instead, and we quibbled good-naturedly over it. But the important thing was that he loved me, faith and all, and wanted to be with me whenever he could. Still, he had been able to meet me only once outside the Bureau for any reason, and that was the day the crew filmed us at the sidewalk café. So he hesitated before answering. Then the phone rang, and he picked it up. I was late to class so I started to leave, but Jerry, holding his hand over the mouthpiece, called to me, "Darling . . . about lunch. I'll try." I smiled and waved good-by.

"The Hamra! That sounds wonderful!" Violet was saying to me, as I stood there, thinking about Jerry. I quickly smiled and agreed with her, a bit embarrassed that I had been daydreaming in the middle of our conversation. The lights came back on at that moment, so I made my good-bys and traveled down the elevator and out the door toward Jerry's office at the Commodore Hotel.

I ambled lazily down the hill. I was a bit early. I turned the corner, and there was the hotel, with the pack of Lebanese drivers lounging around its entrance waiting to drive their journalists anywhere and everywhere.

Then, as I looked toward the annex doorway across the alley where the news offices were, I saw one of the newsroom office workers standing with Fahd and talking anxiously. They saw me and shouted a strange question: "Sis! Is Jerry with you?"

"No, of course not," I shouted back. Then it seemed like the whole staff was rushing toward me, all of them excitedly saying one thing:

"Jerry's missing!"

I remember now that I didn't doubt it for a second. Jerry was never late. You couldn't be late for television. So when Jerry didn't arrive that morning, the assistant on duty instantly knew something was wrong, and listening to her I knew too. "How wrong?" I thought wildly, but went on listening to her excited explanations. When the first crew returned from the assignment, she reported Jerry's absence. Fearing a heart attack, she said she and a driver had broken into our apartment. But Jerry wasn't there, so they had come back to the Bureau. Then I appeared. Maybe Jerry was with the other crew on assignment, someone suggested. Then almost immediately the other crew returned. Jerry was not with them. I remember that someone had already used the word *kidnaped*, and no one questioned the possibility.

The next few hours are a blur in my mind. I remember rushing to the hospitals, struggling with my languages, begging anyone who spoke English to help. I saw every list of new patients, alive or dead, for the last week. Then I went to the police. That visit I recollect with a dull pain that would stay with me for weeks. The police station was, like every-thing in Lebanon, in a state of perpetual chaos. The burly man behind the counter would not even fill out a missing persons report for forty-eight hours. He hinted broadly that Jerry might have had an "assignation."

"He'll tire of her soon," he grunted, coyly smiling. Then with a wave of his hand, he dismissed me and turned to a man who'd lost his car.

Somehow I managed to get back to the CNN offices. I had paused long enough to call Violet before I rushed to the hospitals, and now she came running to me. And behind her were six of my British friends from church, led by Peter Crooks. I can still see their coats and ties, and their dignified manner. One of them was Donald Marston, a former first secretary to the British embassy in London. I sank into one of the chairs.

"People keep using the word *kidnaped*," I mumbled.

"Sis," Donald began, sitting down close to me, "on any given day, there are more than two thousand Lebanese being held hostage in this country. There are actually centers to help their families cope. Kidnaping is almost a way of life here. You can pay a bit of money, and someone will do it for you. There are so many factions with so many agendas. Des-perate measures of a desperate people. . . ."

I was suddenly thinking of the night of the siege when Ed Kellermeyer tried to explain Lebanon's rage to me. The cycle of action, reaction, strike, retaliation—but those were mili-tias. It wasn't supposed to touch us. Then I remember some-one mentioning David Dodge, a former president of Amer-ican University of Beirut, who had been kidnaped nearly two years before, held in Iran, and finally released not too long before we'd come. It had been big news in Beirut but hardly mentioned in America.

Then the talk had changed to Malcolm Kerr, the late president of the American University of Beirut who had been killed on campus, shot to death outside his office by two men posing as students. I remembered the story Jerry had done on it. And now Jerry. . . .

It was touching us. We were vulnerable.

Donald was still speaking. "It's not unheard of for someone to pay to have a person kidnaped just to make a point. Other Americans have been picked up and then set free after only a few hours, sometimes for money, sometimes just on principle."

"That's happened with other newsmen here," someone was saying. "I know that for a fact. They just haven't talked about it."

"But some of them kidnap to sell too," someone was whispering, perhaps so I might not hear. "They sell them to the factions for bargaining purposes, you know. . . ."

I winced, closing my eyes tightly. I ignored the voice. I was grasping for calmness. What do I do next? I must not panic and do the wrong thing.

"Sis," said the British ambassador's secretary, Elsa MacIntosh, "the ambassador thinks you should go immediately to Nabih Berri for help." I looked around at every one of these friends. They were all nodding in agreement.

I began to think, "Could it be? *Could* Jerry have been kidnaped? And if it had to be true, could the kidnaping be *personal,* as Donald was saying? If so, could we get him back quickly if we did the right things?"

Then I began to think about who would do such a thing, if that was it. As a reporter, Jerry had come in conflict with all sorts of personalities, some quite dangerous. Also as the new bureau chief, he had been sent over to straighten out three areas—editorial, administrative and financial. Jerry had told me there were funds that had not been accounted for, a large amount of funds, and there were more people on the payroll than thought necessary by CNN's Atlanta head-quarters. All this Jerry had told me in confidence before he left.

Supposedly, his "tightening-up" duties as the new bureau chief were secret. But within a day or two of his arriving, he discovered that practically the entire American journalists' community knew. But still, within only a handful of weeks, Jerry found out what happened to all the money, cut down on the number of free-lance cameramen, soundmen and drivers, most of them Lebanese, and in a memo to his bosses described offers made to him—which were first-person lessons in how considerable, unethical income could be earned in wartime.

So, to many, *many* people here in Beirut, Jerry was a less-than-popular character from the moment he arrived. Enemies could be made by being honest.

Could this all be somehow connected?

I gazed around again. My friends were still nodding. "Fahd," I called. Fahd had been sitting close by, looking as if he could bite nails in two. "Can you take me to Nabih Berri . . . now?"

He leaped from his chair and grabbed my arm excitedly. "Now—Sis," he said. "Now!" And we ran down the steps.

The ride to Berri's Amal headquarters was as wild as all my rides with Fahd. But this time his speed and his close calls didn't scare me. I was probably in shock. Maybe Fahd was too. We roared up a hill to a residence I'd never seen before.

"Muhammad, my brother-in-law," he explained. "He'll get us in to see him."

I found out that Muhammad, Fahd's massive brother-in-law, was also the brother-in-law of Dr. Ghassan Siblani, Nabih

Berri's right-hand man. And it was Muhammad who called Siblani for permission to come immediately to Berri's military headquarters.

The halls of the house that Fahd and Muhammad took me to were dark and smoke-filled. At the first checkpoint, bored-looking soldiers in khaki uniforms stopped us and told us to check our guns. Muhammad surrendered several. They all seemed to know who he was. I was struck by how casual it all seemed to be. I followed Fahd and Muhammad, feeling as vulnerable as a child. No one seemed to think it odd that an American woman was walking down these long corridors with two Lebanese men.

They led me into an open, spacious room filled with small groups of Arab men, all sitting on ottomans and long sofas, many smoking from dangling water pipes and fingering prayer beads. The walls were draped in curtains from floor to ceiling and the smoke hung in the air. Marching boldly forward through the crowd, Fahd pushed one man from a sofa and gestured for me to sit.

Almost immediately, Dr. Siblani came in. He was a middle-aged man, dressed in a modern suit. He strode over to us, grasped my hand and kissed me on my cheeks three times, on the left, then on the right, then on the left, in Arabic fashion.

Then he said, "We abhor kidnaping. Jerry is our brother. He's been reporting our story fairly. Nabih Berri has commissioned me to find him. We will cordon off the city, and we will get him back. These kidnapings are a stain on us all."

I felt a flood of relief. My legs began to tremble. We talked for a few more minutes before Fahd and Muhammad escorted me back down the long halls where Muhammad had checked his guns. Then, with both of them gently taking my arms, they tucked me in the back seat of Fahd's Mercedes, and we drove away. I laid my head on the back of the familiar seat, thought how odd it felt for Jerry not to be sitting beside me and listened to them chatter excitedly in a language I could not understand.

"Thank you, my friends," I murmured, as the car sped back to our apartment.

We made several attempts to contact the American Embassy to no avail. They did not return our calls. So I was praying hard that Nabih Berri might bring this nightmare to a quick end.

I found out quickly, though, that my foray into Amal headquarters might not be considered appropriate from an American perspective.

"Now you've screwed up," one of Jerry's news staff told me.

"What?" I said. "What do you mean?"

"You went to Nabih Berri."

"So?"

"Sis, from the American government's point of view, he's the enemy."

Our government backed the Maronite Christian government, and Nabih was a Shiite Muslim, so I had just made a formal request of the "enemy." Therefore, my going to see Berri would put me in a bad light with my State Department from the beginning. But I did not care at that moment. I wanted to believe it would all come out right.

When I got back to the apartment, Joan Crooks, my missionary friend, was there. She had cooked me a hot meal and told me she was staying the night. I called my brother, Francis Hare, Jr., a trial lawyer in Birmingham, whom I've always called simply "Brother." He'd already seen a report on television and called CNN, who had told Brother we should not say anything to the press for fear it might hurt Jerry. Brother told me he would begin making calls to try to make contacts for help. He also said that he'd already begun trying to contact the State Department and would call me back.

Then, I told him everything I had done and everything that I knew. I told him what my British friends said and about my sudden suspicion that perhaps this was a personal situation more than a political one.

"Things like that have happened before in Beirut, everybody says," I went on. "I mean, it could be some sort of vengeance for the things Jerry has been doing to straighten up the Bureau's finances. . . ." I felt my voice trailing, almost pleading for that to be the truth. I tried not to think about David Dodge's year-long kidnaping ending in Iran. And I *would* not think of Malcolm Kerr's murder. Jerry was a newsman, I kept thinking. Why would terrorists kidnap a newsman? The press, it's supposed to be safe—safe! Brother was saying something to me, and I forced myself to listen closely.

"Let's pray you're right," he was saying. "But I'm still going to make calls, and I'll get back to you very soon."

The moment I hung up, the phone began ringing. And it kept ringing all night. Every call was from a reporter. I told all of them the obvious facts they already knew, but very little else, asking them please not to write much. Several had actually heard of Jerry's confrontations over the Bureau's financial irregularities and quizzed me about them, hoping to find their own angle for the kidnaping. I could not bring myself to tell them more than the basics, and I repeatedly told them not to quote me without going through Jerry's boss. Although I found it a bit odd that a news network would want to keep a story quiet, I did worry that somehow it might hurt Jerry. So I took the advice CNN had given my brother.

Late in the evening, I finally got a call through to my mother. She was not in good health, and I was worried how she would respond. There had been quite a lot of tension between my family and me over my marriage to Jerry, and that weighed heavily on my mind too. But what I said came from somewhere deep inside.

"Mama, I'm scared."

"Come home," she said.

"No, I've got to stay. I can't leave him." I told her of Brother's plans and left it at that. When I put the receiver down, I felt weak. I was suddenly shaking. "Joan!" I called to my friend in the other bedroom, "Joan! . . . I . . . I think I'm going to have a stroke." I was twitching all over.

Joan sat down by me on the bed and handed me a drink to help calm me.

"No, you're not," she said, resolutely. Then she helped me under the covers, straightened the sheets over my shivering body, and sat down beside me on Jerry's side of the covers. And as I drifted off to sleep, I could hear her saying her prayers.

.

MARCH 7, NOON

"YOU ARE A SPY!"

For four hours this had gone on. Jerry is blindfolded, lying face up on a bed. He is inside a house, not far from where he was kidnapped. Rough voices have yelled the same accusations over and over. Once more, Jerry answers:

"I am a TV journalist. I'm not a spy!"

"No, you are a CIA spy," a voice hisses into his face.

"I am not a CIA spy."

"Then, you're an Israeli spy," another voice tries.

"Why are you holding me?" he yells.

"Stand up!"

Jerry is led outside and told to kneel. For a very long second, Jerry wonders if they are going to kill him now. Then . . .

"Lie down!"

A gag is stuck into his mouth, and he is wrapped from head-to-toe in brown wrapping tape, so tightly he could feel the circulation to his fingers and toes slowly being cut off. Then hands are grabbing his arms, his waist, his legs. He is lifted up, then shoved onto what feels like a truckbed. The engine roars, and the truck screeches away.

Jerry strains to hear every sound, hoping he can figure out where he is being taken. He knows if the trip lasts about two-and-a-half hours they will probably have taken him to the Bekaa Valley, and his captors will probably be Iranian-backed terrorists—the Hizballah. If the trip is longer, he could end up in Iran.

In a few moments, he no longer hears city sounds. A few minutes later, they are slowly bouncing up mountain roads. After a couple of hours, he feels the roads leveling off. Minutes later, the truck lurches to a stop. "The Bekaa," Jerry thinks, "I'm somewhere in the Bekaa."

Rough hands once again grab him. He is dragged into a building, up stairs and thrown onto a pallet in a tiny room. The tape is unwound, but the blindfold stays on. He feels a chain go around his wrist, and he feels it being pulled tight, attached to something near the floor. It cannot be much more than two feet long.

"Where is my wife?" Jerry says. "Have you taken my wife?"

"Don't worry about your wife," one answers.

"She was killed in an explosion!" another says.

"She has found a new man!" another joins in.

And the voices laugh.

MARCH 16, 1984
BEIRUT/CYPRUS

The next week is even a bigger blur in my memory than that first day. My missionary friends took turns staying with me. It seemed that everyone knew. Mike, the barber who owned a shop three blocks from the apartment, saw me outside one day and said, "Come in, come in, and let us do your hair."

But through most of the week, I stayed close to the phone. It rang all the time, incessantly, especially in the middle of the night due to the time difference between Beirut and the States. I finally heard from the American Embassy, days after Jerry's disappearance. They said they had taken so long to contact me because they had heard I was hysterical. "How odd," I remember thinking. If I had been hysterical, it seemed that would have been all the more reason to get in touch right away. But I thought no more of it. I was still hoping for a miracle through the efforts of that first day—

now ten long days ago. I talked at length with Brother many times. He told me he talked to CNN and the State Department several times, and both had warned us to continue to avoid speaking to the press.

"Sis," he said in our first 4:00 A.M. call, "the State Department is saying that the longer Jerry's held, the more chance he's alive. If they were going to make a statement by killing Jerry, they'd have thrown his body out in the streets this first week. They say that means they are keeping him alive for some reason. And CNN just wants us to keep quiet." I could tell by his tone he was as frustrated as I with such talk. "Sis," he said, "we'll keep quiet as they told us to, but we'll do our own thing too."

And he'd begun to tell me about connections he was already making through friends who might help us.

By this time, I needed to rely on someone else so badly, to "coast" for a while, that I remember saying, "You're in charge. Tell me what to do." He told me then that he would fly to Cyprus within the week. He chose Cyprus because the family made him promise he would not go into Beirut. Cyprus was a Middle East "listening post" for journalists and diplomats where stories about Lebanon often originated during that time, but especially later when the situation in Beirut became even worse. "Meet me there in a week, and we will strategize," he said. And I agreed.

So that first week, as reporters called, I was torn between wanting them to tell the story and worrying they might make things worse for Jerry. So I said very little, referring them to CNN in general and, specifically, to Ted Turner, CNN's founder. That's the line I used over and over. Even to the reporters who had somehow heard about the rumored conflicts surrounding Jerry's financial-watchdog role. I wanted to do what I thought Jerry would want me to, and that would be to do what CNN told me.

During that first week, the CNN staff asked me if I wanted to be interviewed for broadcast. I told them I would if they wanted me to. They began setting things up; then suddenly they did not call back.

Meanwhile, Ed Kellermeyer and I went through Jerry's papers, ledgers and calendar and found several things that puzzled us, memos and the like, which confirmed the financial troubles he'd been sent to clean up. We also found out later he'd had one phone threat but had shrugged it off characteristically. He certainly had not told me. We were also confused why the staff felt they had to break in and climb through the window when both Ed Kellermeyer and the landlord, Mr. Ghannoum, were at home.

The next day, I called Atlanta by transatlantic phone and asked for Ted Turner. Jerry's boss, Burt Rheinhart, president of CNN, came on the line instead. I remember the scene, there in my apartment. At that time, I was still clinging to the hope the kidnaping was a personal thing. If it were political, it seemed out of my reach, out of everyone's reach. But if it were personal, and Nabih Berri acted fast as he'd promised. . . . I wanted something done, and I wanted something done now. The man I loved more than life was gone, and I had no idea whether he was dead or alive—although I could never bring myself to consider, through the whole ordeal, that he was dead. And as I talked with Burt, I still wanted desperately to believe that the situation was something that CNN could handle, maybe from within.

During the call, Burt told me that Ed Turner, CNN's number-two man, was coming soon, and to do nothing and say nothing until he had a chance to take over. He explained to me what they had done so far. They had called Washington, sent people to the Syrian and Lebanese embassies, and talked to the United Nations delegates from Saudi Arabia, the PLO and Libya. And they had made calls throughout Beirut, finding out about earlier episodes involving newsmen who had been detained for short periods of time and how their stories had been kept quiet. Many of the newsmen in the city had already called me with such stories, backing up what my British friends had said. Burt told me he had people in Beirut trying to find out anything they could about those stories.

I remember I kept suggesting that it wasn't political, but personal. Didn't it seem quite possible, I asked, praying it was true, that Jerry's disappearance might have something to do with the problems Burt sent Jerry over to fix?

To my amazement, though, Burt quickly responded by saying that he did not know what I was talking about.

That shocked me. Was he "stonewalling" me? And then I remember my abrupt reaction. I asked: Did he *want* me to talk to some of the reporters who kept calling, such as the ones from "60 Minutes" and *Time* magazine and the *New York Times?*

Looking back, I understand that this may have been the worst thing I could have done. From that moment on, I was characterized as being "hysterical" in CNN's eyes. But in spite of the false labeling, I knew it was essential that I remain calm in order to pursue every possible avenue for Jerry's release.

Yet, it was already too late, no matter how any of us behaved. All too soon it would become apparent that even if the kidnaping had begun as a personal vendetta, the situation had escalated to the political level within hours.

We would find out that the group holding Jerry was looking for Americans for their own reasons, big ones. Far bigger than CNN would be able to handle. Yet this one early talk with the president of Jerry's company began a long, strained relationship with CNN—one marked by silence, almost unbearable silence, that would last through the long, long ordeal.

On March 16, nine days after Jerry disappeared, another American was kidnaped. William Buckley, a CIA agent working as a political officer with the American Embassy, had been pulled from his car. Were the men who took Buckley the same ones who had kidnaped Jerry? That day I left for Cyprus, still hoping that Nabih Berri or CNN could straighten this whole situation out quickly. There was no way I could know that it had gone far past the stage where either could have helped.

Nothing happens quickly in the Middle East, my Lebanese friends told me over and over. They are a patient people and expect you to be. As I left for Cyprus, Salim, my kind and gentle driver, quietly advised me, "You must make a friend of time." I faintly knew at that moment how true his words would be.

I took the ferry to Cyprus. I had talked Mr. Ghannoum, my landlord, into allowing Hana to accompany me by promising I would take her no further than the hotel in Cyprus where I'd meet Brother. And Hana was a wonderful comfort and delight. Again, by providing Hana's calming presence during those days, Mr. Ghannoum offered me another invaluable present.

My neighbor, Ed Kellermeyer, promised to hold the fort in Beirut until I could return in a few days. "I won't let you miss anything," he promised. I packed only a small bag because I thought I'd soon be back.

The days that followed in Cyprus with Brother were filled with phone call upon phone call. My brother took over with a vengeance, putting together what we called our "team." But soon the phones proved to be even less reliable than the ones in Beirut, and Brother became frustrated.

"Sis, I can do a better job from home now. And there's nothing else you can do from here, either. Come home with me."

At first I said no. But I couldn't go back to the apartment now anyway. In a phone call to Hana, Mr. Ghannoum had sent word that CNN's Ed Turner had moved into our CNN-leased flat. And I had decided to rely on Brother's lead. I also knew that I could either work with Brother wherever he was, or I could wait in terrible anxiety somewhere in Beirut. So I agreed. Reluctantly, but I agreed.

As I put Hana on the ferry back to Beirut and her family, I gazed across the water to where Jerry was . . . somewhere.

I watched the water part as the ferry moved away from the dock, and I watched Hana waving to me slowly, sadly.

Then I gazed past her toward Lebanon. And I heard my-self speaking to the wind, "I'm not abandoning you, Darling. I *am* coming back."

APRIL 1984

FOR ALMOST A MONTH NOW, Jerry has been in the same tiny room in solitary confinement, chained night and day to a radiator. The chain is so short he cannot stand, his leg muscles have begun to cramp horribly, and there is little he can do about it. The room is bare; the lone window has been painted over. He is told not to try to look out. He has not seen a human face since March. When his captors want to come in the room, he must put his blindfold on. One man repeatedly walks up to him, sticks a gun to his temple and pulls the trigger. Click. Empty. "Blindfold okay, you okay." he says. "You see out, we kill."

They are young. He knows that from their hands and their feet, all he can see of them from the tiny slit at the bottom edge of his blindfold. One has jumped on his legs repeatedly. The others slap him around. They come sporadically. But mostly, he is alone.

The hours have blurred—the days too. So he has begun to scratch a tally on the wall. It is Day 28. As the long, quiet days melt away, he is beginning to worry what effect the silence, the awful interminable silence, will have on him. All he has is his mind for company, and he is beginning to worry whether he will lose that. . . .

The guards appear.

"Why are you keeping me?" Jerry asks, just as he has again and again.

"You spy."

"You know that's not true. I'm a TV journalist."

The hands leave a piece of cold, flat, unleavened pita-like bread, two wedges of tiny foil-wrapped processed cheese, and a glass of hot, sugared tea at Jerry's feet. Breakfast. Once again, he thinks of Sis. "What has happened to my wife?"

This time, there is a pause.

"We do not harm women," the guard answers.

APRIL 1984

BIRMINGHAM

It took us twenty-eight hours to get from Cyprus to Birmingham, Alabama. We missed every connecting flight. On landing in Birmingham, we were greeted by one of my daughters, Florence, who lived near the airport. "Why didn't you telex you were coming too?" Florence was saying, hugging and kissing me. "We've been so worried."

"We didn't know if she was coming till the very last minute," Brother answered, pushing the luggage into Florence's car. I looked slowly around for familiar sights. I had mixed emotions coming back to Birmingham. There were very real ghosts here for me. I loved this Southern city where I was born and lived almost all of my life. Here I had grown up, married young and had five children with my first husband. Now, though, thinking about my past was like thinking of someone else's life. For all those years I had pictured myself the perfect daughter, housewife, volunteer, mother. Then my husband had left me.

Years had past; then I suddenly met Jerry. His career in broadcast journalism had taken him to Birmingham, where he was a television-news director. I met him while working with the Birmingham arts council. With this man, I had been given a second chance, hardly believing it could be true. His long, broad jawline; his raven-black hair; his strong, thick mustache—just seeing them made me feel like a schoolgirl. I knew how very lucky I was to have this second chance at love. We plunged into this wonderful feeling, never wanting to look back. But when it became obvious I was serious about this man so different from us all, the relations with my parents had become seriously strained. My father was a very powerful, old-line Birmingham attorney and judge, and we had always been extremely close. I was his only daughter and first-born child. But when I announced I was going to marry Jerry, he had exploded. Jerry was a Jew. Prejudice dies hard. Soon after our wedding I received a message from my country club, dropping me from their rolls. Then my father fought the marriage in the cruelest way possible—he took us to court to gain custody of my two youngest children, both of whom were finishing high school.

So the memories were not pleasant. And the scars remained, even after my father's death.

"Mama," Florence was saying as we piled into her tiny car. "You aren't going to believe what 'Brother' did." She meant my son, whom we also called "Brother"—"Brother Moss"— much to outsiders' confusion. He was in college in Illinois. "When he heard about Jerry," Florence said, "he actually left school and was stopped at JFK Airport in New York, trying to fly to Lebanon without a passport." I wasn't surprised. He and Jerry had become very close friends, even confidants, over the last few years.

My brother and his wife, Sue, moved me into one of their guest rooms. Immediately, Brother began working the phones, starting to pull together our team. He had contacted the State Department many times and gotten little but the normal urging to keep quiet. When CNN had chosen to speak to the family, they decided to speak only to Brother. When we called, we would be forwarded to their public-relations representative, who only asked us not to speak to the press about Jerry. Years later, Terry Arnold, my State Department liaison, would write that the State Department could get no help from CNN either. We all seemed to be watching each other, to see what we each would do—or not do.

I remember those weeks as ones spent listening. I'd sit on the floor in my brother's home and listen as Brother would talk and talk and talk on the phone. The calls from Beirut always came in the early hours of the morning. At the sound of the ring, I would instantly be alert. I'd pull my bathrobe around me and go down to the end of the hall to Brother and Sue's bedroom. I'd sit outside their door and listen as he made contacts that we all hoped could find Jerry. I became convinced Brother was probably not telling me everything for fear of what I might not be able to handle. The State Department was telling us he was "alive and well"—which became a meaningless catch phrase during the next few months—and was warning us not to do anything for fear of getting Jerry killed.

Slowly and quietly Brother continued to bring our "team" together. Jay Parker, an old friend of ours who was a graduate of the American University of Beirut, volunteered to help. He lived in Washington, D.C., and had put us in touch with a man named George Malouf, a Lebanese-American businessman he knew. George, who grew up in Lebanon, came from a Maronite Christian background. But he firmly believed he could help anyway. To give the team balance, George also enlisted Munir 'Nsouli, a Sunni Muslim and a former Lebanese Ambassador, now retired and living with his sons in Washington, D.C.

George was a fairly young man—large, excitable, energetic and gung-ho. Although he was Lebanese, he was more American in style. And his accent had a French trace to it. He felt he knew enough people in Lebanon, along with those we already knew, that he could help form a network of connections that could watch Beirut for signs of the kidnapers and Jerry.

'Nsouli, a distinguished Arab with the calm repose that career diplomats learn from a lifetime of negotiating, would provide our team with experience and a degree of authenticity. His reputation with U.N. contacts would give us credibility, especially in Lebanon.

Here were two complete strangers from Lebanon who wanted to help. On the day that Jerry disappeared, I remember numbly talking through my shock with my British friends. I kept hearing Donald Marston say, "Desperate measures by desperate people." I kept hearing little Timmy ask, "Who are the goodies and who are the baddies?" And I remember the hate I was feeling—the taste of it, an awful tinny taste that I could not swallow away. I hated more thoroughly and more deeply than I have ever hated before.

"Christian, Muslim, Jew—they're all wrong! They've taken my Jerry," I had said, over and over that awful day, gazing out the window.

And to that, my missionary friend Joan had firmly answered, " 'They' are not Lebanon, Sis, any more than the 'Mafia' is America. Remember that."

Now, here were these two Lebanese, and soon there would

be many more Lebanese friends, Muslim and Christian, trying to get Jerry back from "them."

Sometimes the tension of waiting was unbearable. Sometimes I found myself begging anyone in the family to reas-
sure me. I just wanted to hear that everything would be all
right. I recall now my son-in-law Ray, Florence's husband,
saying softly, "I can't tell you a lie, Sis. I just don't know. But
anything is possible. Anything."

At this terrible low point, I got a lone call from CNN,
asking me all sorts of questions about Jerry's height, weight,
age, next of kin—the kinds of questions Jerry surely had
answered over and over for forms CNN must have had on
file. So finally, I asked the woman what this was all about.

"Oh, this is for the insurance claim," she answered.

Easter drew closer and closer. It was Holy Week, the cul-
mination of the Christian church's high spiritual season
which had begun with Ash Wednesday—March 7. A symbol
of faith that had been so dear to me now only symbolized
my loss of Jerry. I didn't want to think of the spiritual impli-
cations of all that had happened. I wanted my faith to help,
not hinder, what I was going through. But it was getting
harder and harder not to think about the questions I was
constantly fighting back in my mind.

George and 'Nsouli both were talking optimistically about
Jerry being home by Easter. "It is the Arab way—to pick a
meaningful spiritual holiday," George was telling us. "It is
very possible. Everything for the Arab is symbolic—his capture as well as his release." It could happen, we were told.

I wanted to believe. I wanted it all to make sense. Easter.
Yes, that would be wonderful. That would make sense. I
wanted it to make sense.

George had then called to tell us that his "snoops," mostly
children with binoculars climbing trees and phone poles,

had noticed strange behavior going on in a house in West Beirut. He was convinced that was the house where Jerry was being held. Some of Nabih Berri's militia were watching the house, while George tried to find intermediaries to attempt dialog for Jerry's release. Plan B, George said, would be for Nabih Berri's Amal militia to storm the house. I was ecstatic, but I protested loudly against Plan B, worrying about an accident that *could* harm Jerry. We would have to keep waiting.

Then, several days later, my brother sat me down. "Sis, the decision was made to try something, and I didn't tell you about it for fear it would fail." Then he broke the news to me. The group of militia watching the house had stormed it. And they brought out *not Jerry*, but a Professor Frank Regier of the American University of Beirut and a Frenchman, Christian Joubert, both of whom had been kidnaped in February. Within hours, it was worldwide news.

Not Jerry.

I was angry. And I felt guilty for not being happy for Professor Regier. Since I couldn't celebrate for him, and I couldn't allow myself to weep long over this lost chance, I went numb instead. I also knew the storming incident had blown any lines of communication that we might have had if this group was the same one holding Jerry. Regier said he did not know why he was being held and never knew who his terrorist captors were, either.

This strange raid that produced the wrong man was a clue, an ominous one, that perhaps George Malouf was on the wrong track; perhaps he was being fed the wrong information for reasons only the Shiites knew. From the beginning, I had wondered in the back of my mind how a Maronite Catholic would be able to deal with West Beirut's Shiite Muslims dedicated to scaling back Christian political power in the country. Later, I would discuss these problems with Ambassador 'Nsouli when we met in Washington, but for now, in Birmingham, grasping for any good news, I simply could not entertain the idea that George wasn't the best bet we had. And so I didn't.

Easter came and Easter went. And Jerry was not released.

And then, on May 8, another hostage was taken. Reverend Benjamin Weir, a Presbyterian missionary, kidnaped at gunpoint while walking down a Beirut street with his wife.

George reported back. However Jerry's kidnaping had begun, George now confirmed that it was very political indeed. Somehow his connections had found out what group was now holding Jerry, and why. A sect of the militant Shiite radical group Hizballah ("Party of God"), who favored Iranian-style Islamic fundamental rule for Lebanon, was beginning to "warehouse" Americans to exchange for the seventeen Shiite prisoners convicted in Kuwait for bombing the U.S. and French embassies there. Six people had died in the bombings. This much George had heard from his sources, even though it was not publicly confirmed yet. When the *New Jersey* and other U.S. naval ships had begun firing on Lebanon in late 1983, the Iranian-backed Shiite sect had retaliated by attacking the Marines and hitting the American and French embassies in Kuwait. Seventeen were captured. Two of the terrorists were reported to be relatives of several Hizballah members, but they were asking for all seventeen.

"They saw we are at war with them and we should now exchange prisoners. They'll ask for seventeen, but they'll take two," George said. "That's what they do." With that information, we waited. It was all we could do.

Some days I could not move. I was being told I had to keep myself healthy, had to keep a good outlook. "Take lots of Vitamin C," my friends told me. "Keep busy." Keep busy. . . .

At what? Finally, Florence persuaded me to drive to her home outside Birmingham and spend the night with her and Ray and my young grandson Matthew.

And so we fished for catfish from their pond and played a silly game of poker, and then Matthew, to my delight, snuggled down for the night on the sofa with me. And as he fell asleep while I brushed his blond locks from his warm forehead, I could actually feel a chemical change in me. For that moment, my depression lifted. And for the first time in a month, I said a prayer that wasn't one of pleading. Instead, it was one of thanks for that little boy. I could honestly thank God for him, and that wonderful fact crowded out all others—if for only a moment.

After that night, I knew I couldn't just sit by and listen anymore. I had to feel I was doing something, anything.

Then a friend called and said, "Sis, I had the hardest time finding you. CNN was no help. They said, 'CNN has no idea where to contact Mrs. Levin.'" Then more and more friends called with the same story. What was happening with CNN? They *knew* where I was. Why were they acting this way? Were they worried I would embarrass them? Or sue them? They knew Brother was a trial lawyer, well known for negligence cases. Could that be it? I had no idea. But my friends' calls convinced me, more than ever, that it was time for me to stop sitting and wringing my hands—at least here in my brother's home.

My heart was in Beirut, and that's where I wanted to go. But if I could not go back to Lebanon (and the most persuasive argument my family had for my not going back was "What would Jerry want?"), then I'd go back to Washington, if only to meet the people we were working with, and to try to make progress with the State Department. At least the phone calls would be local.

So I began to pack. My family put up only a small fuss, because they too knew I needed to go. My sister-in-law Sue had quietly called my friends Barbara and Margaret, both of whom I'd known for years, to try and talk me into staying. So, as I came down the stairs on the day before I left, there was Margaret.

"Where are you going to go?" she asked, stopping me in my tracks.

"Washington. But I don't know where in Washington just yet," I sighed. "Our house is leased out, but I'm sure we have friends who won't mind having me for a while. After all, I've got a daughter in school there. Clare will help."

Suddenly tears welled up in Margaret's eyes. "Help *me*," she said quietly.

"What?" I said, a bit taken back.

"Help me say the words that will keep you here. I . . ."

Looking at my much-loved friend crying, I recognized the same strong chemical change rush through me that I had felt watching my grandson sleep. It was a relief not to think of my own problems for a few seconds, to be pulled out of myself as I worried about my friend.

"Good grief, Margaret," I scolded quickly, "you'll ruin that silk blouse." And I guided her to the kitchen where, to my surprise, Sue and my friend Barbara were sitting waiting for us, looking worried.

"Okay . . ." I teased, hands on hips, looking at all of them. Nobody said a word. "Well," I finally said, "what do we have to eat around here?"

"You know," Barbara smiled, jumping to her feet, "I just happen to have five pounds of fresh jumbo shrimp. . . ." And so we all experimented making sauces and laughed a lot, finally producing a wicked remoulade. For the first time since Beirut, I enjoyed eating. I can still remember my surprise at how good everything tasted. And then, as a going-away present, with all of us sitting around Sue's kitchen table, Barbara, an accomplished soprano, suddenly began singing my favorite aria from *Madama Butterfly,* "Un Bel Di"—the one with the lovely words that promised "he'd come . . . one fine day."

The next morning I drove to Washington.

MAY 1984

*THE CAPTORS HAVE MOVED Jerry to another "safe house."
But things are essentially the same—the short chain, the dirty
pallet, the solitary room. This time the windows are shuttered
instead of painted. He has not seen another face or a tree or even
the sun since March.*

*The silence is almost unbearable. For days now, he has been
forcing himself to keep mentally alert. He has been doing lists in
his head. Lists of professional football, baseball, basketball and
hockey teams. The names of their stadiums and arenas. The play-
ers on his favorite team, the 1945 World Series champion Detroit
Tigers, each player's position, each player's name. Every opera he
has seen performed, in the order he saw them. And he has replayed
every moment of his courtship and marriage to Sis over and over,
clinging to those precious moments. He searches for places and for
people to think about, ponder—anything to fill the void, to "escape," if only for seconds.*

*But still, he is beginning to talk to himself, and that terrifies him.
It seems the first step toward madness. He has to talk, though. To
whom? To his guards? Hardly. To . . . God? He didn't believe in
God. How could he talk to him? But he must talk. He must. But
prayer? Being an atheist, prayer had always seemed an absurd,*

valueless act, the people doing it fooling themselves. They weren't talking to this "thing" called God. They were simply talking to themselves. . . . Yet they hadn't gone crazy. . . . No. He had no right. Not unless he believed one hundred per cent.

Yet this silence is so thick, unbearably thick. He must *hear the sound of his voice. He* must *sort out what has happened to him. Put it into some sort of acceptable context.*

Groaning, Jerry moves a bit on his pallet to relieve the pressure of the constant lying or sitting position he is forced to stay in. He has lost weight, lots of it. Since the chain is so short he cannot stand up, except for the one time in the morning when they unlock the chain and lead him to the bathroom. In this house his room is close to the bathroom. And inexplicably, they have begun to leave him alone during his daily visits there. It is almost time for today's trip.

The guards enter. Jerry pulls on his ragged blindfold, and they unlock him and lead him the short distance to the bathroom. Inside, alone, he pulls his blindfold off and moves to the bathroom's window. It is painted over. Glancing briefly back toward the door, Jerry scrapes a little of the paint away with his fingernail. He can see mountains. He stares at the sight. It is indescribably beautiful.

When he thinks he's taken enough time, he knocks on the door and replaces his blindfold; the guards lead him back to his room. Then, sitting there in the silence, he suddenly hears what sounds like others being led, one at a time, down the corridor to the bathroom. He hears their knocks to be let out.

He is no longer alone.

The guard plainly says, "Come." He is speaking English.

"Other Americans," Jerry realizes in helpless horror.

MAY-JUNE 1984
WASHINGTON, D.C.

Driving to Washington seemed somehow right. I wasn't even sure where in Washington I was going as I drove, but the act of going made me feel good. At the outskirts of the city, I steered like a homing pigeon toward Jack and Sally Nevius's house. Maybe it was because I had left Washington to go to Beirut from their house, maybe not. But for whatever reason, I simply found myself there, standing unannounced on their doorstep. Maria, their maid, smiled at me as though it were only yesterday that I'd left. Without a word, she put her arms around me for a long moment and then led me down to their secluded guest room.

All through May and June, I stayed with Sally and Jack and their daughter, Kristina, tying up their telephone. The Neviuses were close friends; their daughter is my godchild. Sally even bought me a long cord that extends the telephone into the bathroom and another one that let me take the phone out to the pool.

In those first few days I began meeting the men on our team, and also making my presence known at the State Department's "Lebanon Desk." Between calls from Brother, George and 'Nsouli—who were still at work trying every angle in Lebanon, checking every "exit," as they put it—and meetings with officials, I spent a large part of my time floating in the pool's pleasant water. And as I did, I kept remembering how as a child learning to swim, I was told by a camp counselor that "floating is like becoming a believer. You simply cast your body onto the water, let go and trust." The hours spent floating in the Nevius's pool were quiet hours spent relearning how to "float." I had done it back then, and it had worked. I needed to make myself do it now.

One of the few people in Washington who knew from experience what I was going through was Penne Laingen. Penne had been a Virginia girls-college classmate of mine, and her husband, Bruce, was a career diplomat who had been one of the many Americans held hostage those 444 days in Teheran during the end of the Carter Administration. We spent lots of time together.

"Lots of Vitamin C," Penne said over and over. "And be careful at red lights. I found myself running them often! You'll be so easily distracted. Once," she laughed, "I sprayed my hair with furniture polish and ran out to a meeting."

One worry I didn't expect to have was my credit. I had called all our credit-card companies and our insurance agents and told them about Jerry being kidnaped, with, of course, his credit cards in his pocket. I knew that the card numbers had to be changed and the invoices checked. But the Beirut invoices were never located and so computers kept showing me as non-paying. We found out later that Jerry had had his life-insurance-bill payment in his pocket, too, when he was kidnaped, so it never got mailed. The whole credit-card mess was disconcerting and distressing, to say the least. One of the worst moments was the time I was eating in a restaurant and a waitress asked me for my card and then cut it up in front of me. I limped out, humiliated and drained. I would get calls almost monthly from most of those credit-card and insurance companies asking for Jerry. I'd then suggest they read the next paragraph on their print-out.

"Kidnaped," they would read to me. And then I'd usually hear a tentative, "Oh."

All the confusion of canceled insurance and overdue payments was the natural result of a computerized society not programmed for kidnapings or closed airports in countries under siege which cannot deliver forwarded bills. But there was nothing natural about the way it made me feel. It was a hassle I did not need, but it continued to happen over and over, the entire year.

Then George Malouf called with information that I would use as an anchor for the whole summer. He convinced me that his snoops had redeemed themselves by locating Jerry "for sure" this time. "He is alive and well in Beirut, and our snoops can see him when they bring him out into the courtyard," George went on. "He has lost weight, but he jokes with his captors, and they like him. They say there are only three captors."

Soldiers would again be paid to watch the house until we could negotiate. These were things I wanted to believe, as did Brother. So we believed. During those two months, I always told the State Department what 'Nsouli and George relayed to us. Now George and 'Nsouli were hearing about William Buckley and Benjamin Weir too. Brother and I, and even friends who knew Secretary of State George Shultz, tried every connection we knew, but we could never get a meeting with anyone higher up in the ranks than the State Department's "Lebanon Desk," so we told our information to the "Desk." The State Department didn't disagree with any of the information and continued to tell us the same thing—he was alive and well, but warned in no uncertain terms that if I did not keep quiet and leave the whole affair to them that I would "get the hostages killed." I was assigned a string of "liaison officers" who had little else to offer, sometimes not calling for weeks on end. I was plainly an inconvenience, the first two or three officers actually admitting to me that their orders were simply to baby-sit me and never share any information.

Finally, they assigned me a gentle and experienced man named Ryan Crocker who knew the Mideastern mindset, spoke fluent Arabic and had worked on the David Dodge case in Beirut. Dodge finally had been brought out of Iran in 1983. It was reported but never verified that Syria had brokered for his release somehow. I remember hearing the story while in Beirut, especially on the day Jerry was kidnaped, and now it seemed even stranger to me that the whole affair was hardly written about. But as the days went by, and I noticed that editors across the country were giving very little space to the growing hostage situation, I continued to wonder what was going on. The media people I knew—cameramen, soundmen and reporters—told me often of their frustration. They wanted to dig at the story. The problem, then, seemed to be at a higher level. Somehow, the State Department, in selling their "quiet diplomacy" policy, had convinced these editors that they might harm the hostages by giving them headlines. That was exactly what I was told on the day of the kidnaping, and it was exactly what I had told reporters myself . . . at first.

I was beginning to wonder, though, how not allowing the

public to know what was going on could help the situation. The public's right to know was a conviction that my newsman husband lived by. Things did not seem right, and later many articles would be written in professional journalism journals, as well as a few magazines, about the odd situation. "The Forgotten Hostages," the captives would be pegged before the year was out.

As for CNN, at the time I had no idea if they were doing anything, since they were still keeping up their silent treatment. Neither Brother nor I could get Ted Turner to return our calls. Even the State Department complained that they were unable to reach Ted. But Brother heard he had been quoted as saying, "Do whatever it takes to get him out."

Months later, I learned that CNN had tried quite a few things at the beginning. Back in March, they had reportedly offered $5 million for Jerry, with no takers. Then they'd offered free air time for the kidnapers to air their grievances, which seemingly smacked their allegiance to the "quiet diplomacy" policy in the face. No one responded to that either. Then I found out that they had played a part in financing the raid by Nabih Berri's Amal militia that freed, not Jerry, but Professor Regier and the French engineer Joubert—and when the soldiers had not produced the man they paid for, CNN had demanded their money back and got it!

We were all still doing our own thing. Friends would ask, "What is President Reagan doing? What is CNN doing?" and I couldn't answer. During those long, awful months, I never knew. I had no idea whatsoever what anyone was doing except us. The silence was devastating to me, especially the silence from Jerry's company. As I kept swallowing my anger and my frustration, I was trying to remember how to float.

Then, one day, after several weeks of care and comfort from the Neviuses, I felt I would sink, and sink like a stone.

I was in the process of moving my few things into my daughter Suzelle's empty townhouse on Capitol Hill, which she had not sold since her move out of D.C. We both agreed that it would look better with a tenant and perhaps I could help sell it. That afternoon, though, I had an appointment at the State Department to visit Ambassador Reginald Bartholomew, U.S. Ambassador to Lebanon, at the State Department. He had just returned from Beirut and had met with President Reagan. Jay Parker and George Malouf agreed to meet me at the State Department and accompany me because I did not trust myself to speak unemotionally to him. I could not forget that it was the British Ambassador's staff who had come to my aid on the day that Jerry was kidnaped, and not my own American Embassy. But I knew I needed to make the contact now, and without bringing my emotions into it.

My first indication that I was about to be told something horrible was the sight of George Malouf. This big, hulking man looked like he had been crying, and Jay Parker looked just as distressed. Jay led me to a secluded corner of the State Department lobby and told me the bad news. The Kuwaitis had set a date for the execution of the Lebanese prisoners condemned to die for the bombing of the French and U.S. embassies.

These were the prisoners that the Hizballah kidnapers holding Jerry and the other hostages reportedly wanted in exchange for them. And both the Reuters News Agency and U.P.I. wire services had run stories which had said that the Hizballah had promised to execute their American hostages if the Kuwaiti government executed their condemned prisoners. And then Jay told me, "Kuwaitis have never been known to stay an execution," and I felt a chill rush through my whole body. And as I stared blank-eyed at him as we sat there in the flag-filled State Department lobby, Jay hurriedly told me that he and George had spent the morning searching out contacts to Kuwait in order to plead for time, just in case the Hizballah meant business with their threat.

Struggling for control, I passed through the surveillance gate and walked down the marble foyer to the elevators with Jay and George, and then we were ushered in to see Ambassador Bartholomew. Except for the apologies the Ambassador offered for the Embassy's silence in the days after Jerry was kidnaped, I remember little about that meeting. But there was little to remember. We all four smiled and told each other exactly nothing.

"Jerry is alive and well," the ambassador said.

Beyond that he told us he knew nothing for certain.

So we left. As we stepped outside, the sky grew black and threatening. A storm was about to break.

"Sis, are you sure you're all right? Can you drive home?" Jay asked loudly over the wind.

"Yes," I told him. "Yes, I'm fine," I lied.

"Go home, and wait to get our call. We'll be scrambling to stop the execution. Trust us," Jay said, just as the clouds opened, and the rain came pelting down. I ran down the street to the parking lot, almost unable to see in front of me because of the hard rain. As I ran past a huge tree, one of its monstrous limbs fell, crashing by my feet, broken twigs and leaves hurling past me. Inches closer, and it would have crushed me. But that danger didn't really register with me as I jumped into my car and drove much too fast back to Sally's.

As I strained to see through the downpour, I was suddenly aware of a crunchy texture in my mouth. I spit it out into my hand. It was a leaf.

The storm continued until dawn, and I watched it the whole night, waiting for the call. It came. At 7:00 A.M., George called to say they had pulled off a miracle—they'd contacted the Kuwaitis, who had agreed to delay the execution indefinitely . . . until we could secure Jerry's safe release. I hung up the phone, closed my eyes, said a silent prayer of thanks and relief, and fell quietly to sleep.

The next several days I spent finishing my move into my daughter's townhouse. It was in a rough area of Washington, but it was a place to stay. I couldn't impose on my friends any longer. I had little to move, and the house was very, very empty. After installing the phone, I spent the next few weeks walking around in that almost-empty house. I'd watch the dust collect and wouldn't touch it. I watched the grass grow higher and higher, and ignored it. And I relished the quiet. There, if nowhere else, the world was quiet.

'Nsouli and I met during that time. I remember it was after he had returned from a full day of negotiating with Iranian officials at the United Nations to see if they could wield some influence over Hizballah's men holding Jerry. I'll never forget his words. "We are all being held hostage," he said sadly, "not just Jerry."

Then, in the last week of June, Sally decided that a change of scenery would cheer me and began prodding me to go with her to a renewal conference in the mountains of North Carolina. Jerry's and my sixth wedding anniversary was coming soon, July 1, and Sally felt it would be better to spend it away from the city. I hesitated. The idea worried me because I dreaded leaving the phone.

"Go with me. The lodge office at the conference center has a phone. They'll take any calls, and we'll make sure they hold them for us and come find us," she said. "I promise you will not miss a call."

I was still hesitant. "I'll even pop you on a plane in Asheville, if you need to get back in a hurry!" With that, she won me over. I drove into the mountains with her and found myself in an incredibly beautiful place and surrounded by 400 people who began praying for Jerry the moment we met. I'd find little notes stuck under my door and quick, spontaneous hugs from these strangers.

Then one morning, the conference leader began speaking on world affairs, about our moral obligation to learn about and act on the "situation" in Latin America. He was speaking passionately, gesturing vigorously. Suddenly I found myself on my feet, saying, "Yes, of course we should learn more about Latin America! But don't you think we have the same moral obligation to understand the Middle East situation? We should be talking about that! We know so much about Israel, but why not Lebanon? Why not? Don't you think there might be some things to understand about the other point of view too? Something seems to be wrong! Really wrong!"

The place was filled with all 400 people. And yet it was now so quiet; no one even coughed. My legs were trembling, and I heard someone mumble something about "Armageddon." And then the speaker said, "Yes, well, Lebanon. . . . It is a bit like Afghanistan, I guess, so hard to understand . . ." and then tried to change the subject.

"Afghanistan?" I said. "Afghanistan!" And I went on and on. I was out of control. I had lost my temper, and no doubt, any sympathy I'd had before. I don't even remember much of what I said after that, but finally I sat down. And at the very first chance, I left the meeting hall, wanting desperately to go home.

Trudging up the hill to the lodge by myself, I felt awful. I was mad and I was embarrassed, but that wasn't what was hurting the most. It was the feeling of being abandoned— the feeling I'd first felt in that Beirut police station, the feeling I'd felt with a stonewalling State Department and a silent CNN. And now, as I was taking my first hesitant mental steps toward a sane way to help Jerry, some different way, some informed way, I felt it again. Americans know so little about the problems or the people in the Middle East. How could they comprehend what had happened to Jerry?

"Why don't they care!" I said out loud.

Then it hit me: Why *should* they care? I hadn't really cared much beyond simple curiosity myself until the conflict forced itself into my life and took up residence. I needed Jerry back. The thought of him bound and gagged, hurting somewhere far away from me, gave me more pain than I could ever bear. Yet that didn't mean much to a world full of people who are suffering with their own need and pain.

So standing in that pathway in the Carolina mountains, I suddenly saw things very clearly. I realized that by loudly making a fool of myself in front of 400 people, I had learned an invaluable lesson. I realized on that Carolina hill that if I were to make any difference at all to my own need, then I had to connect my need with other people's needs in some way that touches them too. Standing in that meeting hall on trembling legs, challenging that poor, bewildered speaker, I had experienced my first lesson on how *not* to talk about the Middle East problems. I was beginning to understand the importance of listening and the futility of confrontation. I was beginning to understand how peace worked. It was the first of many small turning points that would finally turn my thinking, and my life, in a new and permanent direction.

All those new and somewhat confusing thoughts were going through my mind as I walked up to the desk in the lodge.

"Did anyone call for me?"

"Yes," the lady said. "A man with a foreign accent just called. You just missed him."

I had to get back to Washington and to my own phone, as fast as I could.

JULY 1984

JERRY IS LYING QUIETLY ON HIS pallet, his eyes pressed tightly closed. He is sick, an intestinal virus with all the accompanying effects. It comes in waves, out of control, and he is losing more and more strength each day.

He hears someone at the door. He has just seconds to get his blindfold on before the guards enter. It is now a reflex action. Once a day, a trip to the bathroom; three times a day, a small smattering of cold food or an occasional hot meal. They resent his increasing knocks for extra bathroom trips because of his virus. They grab his arms and lead him out the door.

But, this time, they are not taking him to the bathroom. They turn the opposite way and take him to a different room. A piece of paper is shoved into his hands. He is told to take his blindfold off and look straight ahead. He is staring into a video-camera lens. A voice from someone out of view orders him to read the paper.

"I am Jeremy Levin," Jerry recites. "My life and freedom depends on the life and freedom of the prisoners in Kuwait."

Now, at least, he knows why he is being held. In a few minutes, he is back in his silent room, chained, alone. The door thuds behind him.

"It won't work. The U.S. won't do it," he says quietly to himself. And he is hit by another wave of stomach cramps.

The virus is getting worse. Much worse.

JULY 1984
WASHINGTON, D.C.

On July 4th, my friends Penne and Bruce Laingen invited me to their annual Fourth-of-July picnic. I found myself sitting on a blanket in a circle of Iranian guests spreading delicious but strange foods before me. I tried to be friendly. But I kept feeling the irony of their presence here. How could Bruce feel so comfortable with Iranians that he'd actually have them to his house after his ordeal as an Iranian hostage for those 444 days?

And then I thought of my own Lebanese friends. I thought of Joan reminding me that the people who had taken Jerry were not "Lebanon," and I frowned, confused. I knew she was right, and I knew my Lebanese friends were wonderful, but that didn't change the awkward feeling I had. When Bruce looked at these people, didn't they remind him of that horrendous experience? Wasn't he mad at all? The part of me that loved my Lebanese friends understood; the part of me that hated the Lebanese who took Jerry did not.

Watching Bruce move from group to group, smiling warmly, I thought of the *Stockholm Syndrome*, the psychological expression picked up by the press describing a released hostage's identifying closely with her captors. In the press it had come to mean attempting to explain or understand one's "enemy's" position. Putting a psychological-sounding tag on such behavior allows the public not to take it seriously, to explain it away. That I knew was wrong, but still, I could not shake the part of me that did not want to understand Bruce's interest in these Iranians. Bruce's compassion for the Iranians would later cost him the loss of a much-desired Canadian ambassadorship, several State Department people would tell me.

"It goes with the territory," Penne said when I asked her about it. Then she added, "You'll see."

At that party I met Terry Arnold, number-two man in the Office of Counter Terrorism at the State Department. I guessed that Bruce had invited him just so we'd meet. Terry was slated for retirement, but he volunteered to stay on and be my liaison to the State Department, replacing Ryan Crocker who had been transferred. We became instant friends because he treated me with kindness and patience and interest. We didn't always agree, but we could always talk. And for those first weeks, not once did he say, "Jerry is alive and well," or "just go home and remain quiet." For that alone, I would have been his friend.

The next week, four months after I had left Beirut, I received word that Ed Kellermeyer, my Beirut neighbor and friend, had finally been able to pack all our belongings into our steamer trunks and ship them back to me. I had only to go to a New Jersey warehouse to claim them. I looked forward to the train trip up there, because I had decided to stop in Princeton and visit David Dodge. Although he guarded his privacy, he had graciously agreed to see me. Also, I hadn't seen Jerry's brother, Jud, and his wife, Audrey, since Jerry's kidnaping. They lived near the warehouse, and we needed a visit, so they volunteered to go with me to claim my trunks.

But when we entered the Bekins warehouse, we were greeted by the sight of four large, black metal trunks which from the looks of the locks and the contents, had been forced open and emptied somewhere along their journey onto very dirty ground. Everything was filthy. The customs officer appeared, looked outraged and urged me to make some sort of claim.

Once more, I felt I couldn't think or move. I just stood there watching while Audrey fished out my broken jewelry case, collected scattered pearls and rearranged dirty clothes. Ed Kellermeyer had told me how he had packed my favorite suit, a pink ultrasuede jacket and skirt, in tissue paper and positioned it carefully in the trunk so as not to wrinkle it. It was now in Audrey's hands, smudged and wadded. My throat went dry, and my chest constricted. It was as if I were seeing my life in front of me, in the same sort of shambles.

It took us a long time to get everything straight, but finally I signed the papers to have the mess sent home. I was so depressed. I stayed on the train back home and watched the Princeton stop go by while I tearfully wrote the understanding Dodges that our visit would have to come later. By the time I got back to Washington, it was already dark. As I walked down G Street to the townhouse, I realized that in normal times I would have been frightened to walk alone in this area. But now I didn't care. I just did not care. Without Jerry, there simply didn't seem any difference between G Street and our own safe neighborhood across the city. There was no reason to keep myself safe. Maybe the old fears would return when this nightmare was over, but I felt no fear now. I trudged through the iron gate and the double-lock door and pulled the door shut behind me.

I dropped into a chair and rewound my answering machine. "We have some good news for you," a now-familiar voice announced. The voice was Terry Arnold's. "We have a videotape of Jerry made ten days ago. It came yesterday while you were gone. It is top secret. Come down to the State Department early tomorrow morning. Let's do our talking there."

Top secret or no, I called my son to go with me. He was spending the summer working at my son-in-law's vineyard in the Virginia countryside west of Washington, and I felt I needed him because I knew I might have trouble identifying Jerry. The tape would be bad quality, and Jerry would probably be bearded and haggard. Maybe I couldn't be sure it was Jerry.

I was right. As we watched the tape, I didn't recognize his voice. It sounded soft and weak, and this paralyzed me with anxiety. I looked at my son.

"That's Jerry," he said positively. They ran it a second time. He was dressed in a dark warm-up suit, but I could tell he was desperately thin. His hair was tousled and matted. He didn't have his glasses on, and his eyes looked tired and dilated. But still, although he looked ill, just to see him was wonderful. I felt anxious, and I felt excited. Then I felt anxious again. Had they broken his glasses? His voice was mechanical and flat, and very unsettling.

"I am Jeremy Levin," he said, glancing down at a piece of paper.

"He never calls himself Jeremy," I mumbled. "He certainly didn't write that."

He went on to say that the message was addressed to Ted

Turner, chairman of Cable News Network. Then he slowly read a message: "My life and the life and freedom of the other hostages depends on the life and freedom of the prisoners in Kuwait."

Then Jerry requested that Ted Turner ask our government to intercede in the matter.

Ted had still not answered any of our phone calls, so I wondered what would happen. "Are you going to send this to Ted?"

Terry answered that that was a decision he couldn't make. It was being handled on a higher State Department level. I thought how odd it was that the government would withhold such a piece of information from the man to whom it was addressed. It was like holding up a citizen's mail, wasn't it?

"My greatest concern right now is for your silence," Terry said. "We are in touch with the Algerian government who have agreed to intercede as a third party, Sis. I think I can predict weeks, not months," he said, "but of course I can't promise anything." Such words had become so repetitious that I couldn't pump up one ounce of hope from them. "This cannot leak out, or our plans could be aborted," he was saying.

Leak out? . . . It was beginning to dawn on me that the government was probably just as worried about its image in this hostage crisis as it was in the crisis itself. Why, I realized, this whole hostage situation is probably an embarrassment for President Reagan in this election year. I remembered his promise in the Rose Garden in 1981 after beating Jimmy Carter—whom he defeated in large measure due to the Iranian hostage situation—that America would never be held hostage again. Public awareness of the seriousness of the hostages' plight could be devastating. And I knew the truth.

George recently told us that when his people in Beirut had

finally helped him contact the Hizballah people holding Jerry, they had said they were willing to engage in private human-itarian negotiation such as George and 'Nsouli were suggest-ing. If that were true, would they also deal with the Algerians? George and 'Nsouli were leaving the next night to go back to Beirut. How could I let them go without complete infor-mation? "Terry," I said, "I need some counseling help. I want to call in my brother."

Terry didn't like the idea of enlarging the circle but finally agreed. I called him, and Brother jumped on the next plane to Washington. Later that same day we stared at the tape together. This time, when one of Terry's aides rewound the tape, he rewound it a bit too far, and I noticed another figure facing the camera right before Jerry's clip. It had to be either Ben Weir or Bill Buckley. The aide did not notice that I saw. And I said nothing.

Carefully and methodically Brother told Terry that George and 'Nsouli were leaving that very night to go back for us. All the signs were excellent. 'Nsouli, who had worked through diplomatic channels while George had worked through pri-vate Beirut contacts, had decided that the two routes to go diplomatically were either to contact Iran (who was allied to the Shiite Muslim factions) or to contact Syria (whose pow-erful presence was felt all over the Middle East, especially in Lebanon).

'Nsouli had convinced the Syrian representative at the U.N. that our mission was totally humanitarian. The Syrians were the obvious choice, according to 'Nsouli, because they had a strong influence historically on Lebanon's Bekaa Valley, which was supposedly where the Hizballah's headquarters were hidden.

In his talks with the Syrians, 'Nsouli told them that Jerry's father had been well known for his writings on human rights, and his family had an impeccable history of benevolence and compassion. Jerry's role as an objective journalist telling the Middle East's story to the world also seemed to strike the right chords. And then 'Nsouli tried a tact that will always mean the world to me.

"I will claim him as my brother!" he said. This wise, strong Arab explained proudly that this was a very traditional Arab right, and he was quite convinced his fellow Arabs would honor his appeal. The whole idea was wonderful—a Muslim Arab claiming brotherhood with Jerry, an American Jew, on behalf of his Christian wife. Potentially there was great symbolic value in this. It had to work.

The Syrians telexed London and set up meetings for George and 'Nsouli with other Syrians as well as Iranians, to determine whether they should go straight into Lebanon or go first to Damascus for more consultations.

Listening to all this, Terry first looked startled and then a bit apprehensive. So when I mentioned we would definitely ask for the other two hostages if our method worked for Jerry, Brother suggested that perhaps we shouldn't do that since our plan was obviously a "high-risk alternative" to the government's strategy. Terry answered, "Oh, no, try for them all."

We put George and 'Nsouli on the plane to London that night. It was July 20.

July 21st was a full day and night of nothing but waiting— waiting to hear from London. In the early hours of the morning, listening for the phone to ring, I felt a certain amount of rest and reflection and creative thinking that had strangely become a habit during those long, quiet nights. I couldn't sleep, but, for some reason, I also didn't feel anxious. Perhaps it was out of self-defense, but those quiet times were calm times of thought.

Lately in those long, quiet nights, lying in my bed unable to sleep, I had begun to think about a new idea. Incredulous as it seemed, I wondered if maybe Jerry needed something that only I could give. Was that possible, or was it merely the rambling imagination of a physically and mentally exhausted woman? That was the thought running through my mind over and over as I waited for that call from London.

Then the phone rang. George's first call from London was to tell me that all signs were "go," and he and 'Nsouli both were excited.

"There isn't any reason to go to Damascus, Sis," George said. "We're going on to Beirut and wait for their call. We'll be in contact with Jay, and he'll relay the message to you."

I caught my breath. Then I called both Jerry's father and Jud, his brother. I should have waited, but things sounded so good, and we all wanted good news so very desperately. It sounded so reasonable. Since the time George had told us that his snoops had spotted Jerry in West Beirut, we had believed that all that was left was a matter of negotiating for his freedom.

Jay Parker had left a message for me to go to his girlfriend's for their call about information from George. I had never met his girlfriend, but I did what he said and drove to her house. We waited in the kitchen together, for the wall phone to ring. The call came.

"Now, Sis . . ." Jay began. His voice was definitely strained. I leaned against the wall, the phone to my ear, and tried to breathe deeply. ". . . George has got some bad news." With that I slid down to the floor to keep from falling there. My palms were too sweaty to hold the phone in place. I juggled it, trying to get a grip on it and my composure. His words were terrifying me. Jay's girlfriend stood close by. Obviously he had arranged for me to be with her in case I'd need help.

100

"They've managed to move Jerry somehow."

Move him! How could three men move a captive from a house that had been watched for weeks by soldiers? All this time my one consolation, my one link to sanity and hope, had been that we supposedly knew where Jerry was. He was alive. They could see him. I believed that George had found Jerry when the State Department said it could not. Now, nothing! If it were Jerry, he was gone. If it had not been Jerry.
. . .

Then as if to stop my tears, Jay began quickly to tell me what George and 'Nsouli had planned. They had been able to meet with Sheik Mohammed Hussein Fadlallah, the fundamentalist cleric regarded as the spiritual leader of the loosely aligned Hizballah. He in turn had put George and 'Nsouli in touch with the group holding Jerry.

"So close," I thought. "Could they really be that close?"

George's contact had shown him a new Polaroid snapshot of someone who was supposed to be Jerry. "They want $25,000 for this evidence," he said. "What?" I heard myself gasp. "I don't have that kind of money." Was it really Jerry?

"They let George and 'Nsouli hear the audio portion of the videotape you saw at the State Department," Jay said and then explained that a meeting was set at which 'Nsouli would make his brotherhood claim and the "humanitarian" appeal, and they would report back.

It was too much to take in at one time. Had Jerry ever been in that house in West Beirut? If not, what did that mean? But the meetings with Sheik Fadlallah. That sounded so good, so promising. If 'Nsouli's plan worked, how would he be released? I agonized. What would happen to the other hostages? I had a twinge of guilt over that thought, but I couldn't hold back the desperate thoughts stampeding through my head.

101

I couldn't think another moment. I hung up the phone, my hand clinging to it a long second before I could let it go. Then I thanked Jay's sympathetic friend for being there, and somehow found my way home. The call would come later that day, a conference call between Brother in Alabama, George in Beirut and me in Washington. Again, I was to wait.

Several hours later, the call came. I could tell instantly by Brother's voice that we were nowhere once more.

"They delayed the meeting," he said, sounding very tired. "But we're still optimistic. They'll try again tomorrow."

Tomorrow came. There was no meeting.

"Sis, it fell through," Brother explained when he called me that afternoon. What had happened to us became clearer. He said we were obviously now in a bidding war. 'Nsouli's humanitarian plea couldn't stand up to whatever it was the captors were hopeful of getting from the U.S. government. It was obviously naive of us to expect them simply to let Jerry go.

But what troubled me most were the suspicions I was finally beginning to face about the information we were receiving. Had we been lied to all along? So many things didn't add up. George, who seemed beyond treachery, was telling us that his contacts knew where Jerry was, could even see him. But if so, how could he suddenly disappear? It had obviously turned out to be a lie. A lie I had clung to all summer long. Were they using us, playing us along? When I met with 'Nsouli later, he told me that was exactly what was happening, that the Shiite Muslims were playing games with George—the Maronite Christian, the Lebanese-American. "George was always pushing too much, too fast," 'Nsouli reminded me, adding that this was not the Middle East way, just as Salim, the driver, had told me I must "make a friend of time." So the ones with power were perhaps "yanking our chain" a bit. And perhaps some of our contacts might just be plain using us.

"It is not new," 'Nsouli had said with that kind, sad smile. There were people everywhere who would take advantage of others' pain. We weren't the first or the last. So now we did not know where Jerry was. We probably never knew where Jerry was. I'd no doubt been trusting in a sweet lie all summer, and I couldn't bear to let it go.

"Sis, we're not giving up," Brother was insisting.

"Sis . . . Sis!"

I hung up. I hung up hard on this person who loved me dearly and was helping the best he knew how. It was as if I could shut out the bad news by cutting off the bearer of the news. All I had to do was hang up, and the bad news would go away. And then I called back, and I cried.

My brother and I talked empty words for a few moments, trying to comfort each other over the phone. It didn't work, so finally we said good-by. Then the phone rang again. It was Jerry's life-insurance company. They were calling to tell me that Jerry's life insurance had been canceled. I hung up. That was the one thing I would not think about, that I might actually end up claiming that insurance. The company called back. I answered and calmly suggested they look very closely at their computer screen.

"Kidnaped," the young woman read. There was a pause. "Oh."

The next few days were a blur. I cried often. I didn't talk to anyone for several days. It was like being in limbo. Then George's wife, Suzy, called, frightened because there was no telex from George saying which plane to meet or when. I'd call Brother's office, and they'd tell me they didn't know where he was. It was like I was being isolated again, abandoned. It was too much. I had to get through to him.

George finally called Suzy from London and limped through customs a day later. I went with her and their children to pick him up. "Where's Jerry?" everyone of us shouted at him as he approached us. And then I wished we hadn't. George was very, very sick.

"I'm going back, Sis," he said. "We'll get him out. You'll see."

We took him straight to the hospital. The doctor told us that his pancreas had shut down and that a few more hours' delay would have thrown George into shock. He was to be in bed for two weeks.

Back at home, I found out that I couldn't get through to Brother because he had collapsed at his Lake House and was bedridden too.

I was overwhelmed with guilt. Had I done this to them? I had to leave those two men alone and try to remember how to float again.

I grabbed my Bible and went to the window. I had been answering my nagging spiritual questions by thinking that things were working out. I was part of a stream of details that were flowing, moving, in the right direction. I had known God was doing something with our efforts in the Holy Land and allowing us to be part of some sort of historic part of the whole picture in the Middle East. Maybe our simple, peaceful way could make a change. But now—now we were back to mindless terrorism. Jerry's being kidnaped was once again just a cosmic accident with no meaning at all. No meaning at all! I thumbed through my Bible nervously. I held it in my hands, trying to calm down, but I was gripping it so hard my knuckles went white, as I grew angrier and angrier.

"What is happening? What is this all about? Where are you in all this, God?" I whispered, through clenched teeth. And then I was yelling. "Don't you care? Shouldn't you care?"

And I did something I have never done before. I flung my Bible with every last drop of energy I had. It hit the wall and fell face down onto the floor. And I dropped to my knees and cried for longer than I care to remember.

AUGUST 1984

JERRY LIES DOWN TO REST. *He still can only sit and lie in certain positions because of his chain, but he has not felt like moving around anyway. He is still weak from the virus. After several excruciating days, the guards could not deny he was worsening. He was living in his own stink.*

So a doctor appeared, examined Jerry, then told him he would be given some medicine.

The medicine never came. Jerry continued to get worse through the night and the next several days. Finally, the guards sent for the doctor again.

"Didn't you take your medicine?"

"They didn't give it to me," Jerry whispered, almost too weak to respond.

The doctor barked a few orders in Arabic, then turned back to Jerry and assured him he would be given medicine immediately. Then he paused. "We have nothing against you as person," he said in broken English. "We just hate the New Jersey—we hate America for bombing us and killing our people."

The weeks that followed had been miserable. Only within the last day or two had Jerry felt well enough to think straight. And now, he is thinking very straight—perhaps too straight.

Over and over, Jerry has been running his captor's demands through his mind. And with every second's worth of thought he gives them, they become more terrifying, because he knows they are hopeless. His newsmen's knowledge will not allow him to deceive himself on that account.

So what is left?

Jerry places his hand around the chain binding him to the wall, not wanting to face the answer to that question. He has always been afraid to die, terribly afraid. But he must look at the truth, and the truth is that there is a very real possibility that he will die here.

With that thought, he angrily yanks at the chain. He will have to escape, he tells himself. The thought makes him go cold. He yanks the chain again in frustration.

AUGUST 1984
WASHINGTON, D.C.

The first few days of August I spent trying to think things through, trying to view from all angles what had happened so far. I was moving into a new phase in our crisis, though I wasn't aware of it at the moment. I wouldn't let myself think about any more closed doors.

So I read. I read all I could find on this land and these problems that had shoved their way into my life.

I read, and I talked. I had a dear friend, Elizabeth Aldridge, who is one of those friends who will talk about anything, anything at all. I knew she would allow me to talk through the whole confusing mess without my worrying about how she would react. Elizabeth and I had many long talks during those days. And the hours would fly by as they do when friends talk about things that matter.

I was angry, still so angry it was blinding. The State Department, CNN, the press were not there for me. Now I had my doubts if they were there for Jerry. I'm not sure what I expected. I just know I didn't expect silence. And I found that all silence does is breed anger—the loud kind.

And now our own team's efforts—all for nothing. The result: two exhausted men and a guilt-ridden woman. And my anger was almost overwhelming.

"How does it feel?" Elizabeth asked one day, as we sat on her rooftop patio overlooking Washington.

"It clings down in your guts and comes out to haunt you alone in the dark," I said. "It's a hatred for what is. Things you can do nothing about. And your helplessness to change what *is* grinds slowly through your whole system. And it leaves you feeling weak. Weak and victimized."

"That's what your Ambassador 'Nsouli meant, wasn't it?" Elizabeth said. "You know, when he said we're all being held hostage?"

"Maybe so," I answered. "The anger isn't just a reaction to people, but to situations—"

"Over which you have no control," Elizabeth finished. "What about forgiveness? What would forgiveness do?"

"I don't know. If you could forgive, then you'd be set free of the anger, I suppose," I sighed. "I just know I don't have anything but lip service to give to that idea right now. It's at my very angriest, like right now, that I feel as if I'm crying for a help that does not or will not come, and yet I can't stop myself crying out for it."

"Whom are you crying out to?" Elizabeth asked.

I paused for a moment. " . . . To God, Elizabeth," I said. "Where else but to God?"

We both were quiet for a moment.

"Forgiveness just isn't natural," Elizabeth finally said.

"No, but anger sure is. But it's so crippling and obsessive. We'd be so much better off to get rid of it," I said and then added, "If we just knew how."

"Exactly," Elizabeth said.

"What am I going to do, Elizabeth?" I said, throwing my hands up. "Am I just stuck with my rage, then?"

Rage . . . why did I use that word? It was the word Ed Kellermeyer used during the siege when he was explaining the Lebanese's feeling about U.S. intervention. Yet it was the perfect word for how I was feeling.

A psychologist once told me that forgiveness first must begin with looking at the hurtful situation or person honestly until you understand your own reaction. Almost always, he said, there is a lie that must be discovered or uncovered and then faced before real forgiveness can happen, before you can be free of it all.

Lies?

No lies for Jerry Levin, is all I could think. Whatever his faults, he certainly could not tolerate anything but the truth. Yet they seemed to be swirling all around both Jerry and me. Where do I begin?

Obviously, if I could see more clearly I could think more clearly. Then that would flow naturally into speaking the truth more clearly, even when it's painful. But that would take an objectivity I just didn't have at the moment. I squirmed at the thought.

Our conversation grew deeper. I had just finished reading two books, M. Scott Peck's *People of the Lie* and Colin Chapman's book *Whose Promised Land?*

"You do believe there is evil in the world?" I asked Elizabeth. "Real evil?"

"Do you?" she answered, leading me right back into my own question.

"I feel as if I've got firsthand knowledge," I said.

"What does Dr. Peck say?"

"Well, he believes that most of our modern dilemmas are largely a result of lying. Evil stems from lies we tell ourselves to make ourselves feel better about the hurtful things we believe—such as prejudice."

"Interesting thought," she said. "So then we encourage evil action by disguising such lies, and we may not even know it."

But I didn't really hear her. My mind was off trying to make sense of things again. I remember how the BBC correspondent, Chris Drake, in Beirut, had likened the struggle there as one of Good vs. Evil. Was it that simple? Was it that simple across the Middle East? "Killing themselves for years over the same piece of land," Ed had growled during the siege. Then I remembered the words of Colin Chapman I'd read over and over during those weeks:

> One of the most distinctive marks of a "Christian" response to the conflict over the land should be repentance. Instead of simply pointing the finger of accusation at others, the Christian should be willing to admit the guilt of all the parties in the conflict and say "both we and our fathers have sinned."

Right/Wrong, Truth/Lies, Good/Evil. Retaliation on retaliation. Everybody seemed wrong. Everybody needed forgiveness. For the first time since my small revelation on that Carolina hill in June, I began seriously to consider that there had to be a better way. What had caused Jerry to be kidnaped? Rage? I could hear Ed Kellermeyer talking of rage as we listened to shells explode over our apartment house.

But I could also see Ann Kerr, Malcolm Kerr's widow, being interviewed by Jerry and other newsmen after her husband was shot to death outside his American University office. "Our family is staying in the Middle East," she had said, "to serve the people we love." Rage vs. Love. Even with all my anger, I knew which I'd pick to nurture.

So the silence, and the loud anger created in me that summer, was beginning to drive me forward. And the questions flooded in:

"Why aren't we talking about these problems?" I would ask Elizabeth over and over. "If you can't talk about problems, how can you solve them, Elizabeth? How else can you figure out the old lies that ignite the problems, that make them explode again and again?"

Elizabeth didn't know.

Without words, though, how can anybody be expected to choose reconciliation over retaliation?

All that time, I had been writing in my journal daily to help myself understand my own feelings and to try to make some sense of all the conflicting data about what was happening to Jerry and me. And as I wrote, I began to see a sort of "message" forming. The hostages were only the tip of the iceberg. Maybe we, the general public, were completely missing the point. There seemed to be a desperate cry for help coming from Lebanon. And we, the superpower, were deaf to it. There was a context to the hostages' captivity that was full of history and insensitivity, bad choices and pain. The kind that comes when a nation abandons dialog and embraces military force.

Outside of that context, Jerry's episode made no sense at all, or worse, it could be used to make the kind of sense that served *anyone's* purpose. And I knew that to be true, because I had been one of the misinformed myself.

All of this was quite a revelation for someone who had never made more than a handful of independent decisions in her whole life. But during that month, I had a growing awareness that I might be able to do something for Jerry that no one else was doing. Or maybe that no one else was able to. And, after all, I had the most at stake.

113

During those weeks, I was working up to making a leap that was either very foolish or very wise. During that last part of the summer, though, several things happened that forced me into that jump.

First, as I mentioned, we could not help but fear that our own efforts through our "team" might have reached a heart-breaking dead end. We obviously could go no further in the direction we'd been going. Also, it looked fairly certain that the contacts George had cultivated were only partially trust-worthy. I had waited and listened and answered the phone all those months while George, 'Nsouli and Brother had done the best they could for Jerry and me. Even from those wonderful men, their best hadn't been good enough. I grad-ually began feeling that I wanted to take more responsibility for my own situation and for my husband's. How, I had no idea. What could I do that hadn't been done?

Then, George told me a piece of information that we couldn't ignore. During their meeting with the Shiite group who claimed to be holding Jerry, George had heard one of the men bragging that they would attack the American Em-bassy in East Beirut between September 20 and 22. George and I were both aware that revealing such a piece of inside information might jeopardize Jerry and could definitely af-fect George's on-again, off-again connections with the ones who were holding him. We had no idea if the captor's words were simply rhetorical threats or not. But how could we not warn our government about something like that? Jerry would have cringed at the thought of keeping such a threat a secret. And if it turned out to be false, what would be the harm? If it turned out to be true, lives could be saved, even if that meant we would have to deal with the consequences of our having told the truth—because it was entirely possible that the captors had allowed George to hear their plans because they wanted to test him.

So on August 16, after George had completely recovered, we set up an appointment with State Department officials, including Terry Arnold, at the State Department building. George told them the story. The members of the Hizballah with which he had met had bragged to him they would deliver "a gift-wrapped package" to the embassy "around September 20 to 22." They had said, "We will prove that America is a giant with feet of clay. We'll hit them again where they don't expect it. If they think they're safe in East Beirut, they're not."

When we met with the State Department officials, though, they didn't hide their skepticism. I could tell they were not going to act on the information—which would prove disastrous. As I left, I suddenly felt an overwhelming reluctance to leave Jerry's life in their hands anymore.

Then after only a few weeks, it became deadly obvious that our team would *not* be able to do more.

Ambassador 'Nsouli had not come home with George. He had business in Europe and then wanted to swing back through Lebanon to check things out once more before returning to the U.S. But, in Paris, he received a call from his son in Lebanon.

"Don't come back. You will be killed." Somehow word had leaked that George had told the State Department about the bombing plan. George was now and forever a "spy," and 'Nsouli was linked with George.

'Nsouli, who had spent his whole life working for his beloved Lebanon, would have none of that. It was now a matter of honor. He told his son to tell those in authority who had issued the warning to meet his plane. He was coming back.

When the next plane from Paris landed at the Beirut airport, there was a group waiting for 'Nsouli—his family, and the officials complete with armed guards, who had threatened 'Nsouli's life and reputation. Out strode the distinguished Ambassador 'Nsouli in proud Arabic fashion. He stood in front of the officials and their soldiers, and said loudly, "You know me. You know my service to this country. I will not hide, and I will not run away. I have claimed a man as my brother, and I have done nothing wrong. If you are going to kill me, kill me. But I am here."

And with that, they greeted him back with kisses on both cheeks. 'Nsouli's name was cleared. But that interlude told us that George could never go back—and that perhaps he was being tested all along.

Even my brother felt defeated. A Birmingham news reporter interviewed him while he was recuperating. And in that interview, he said, "She's in charge now." When I read those words, I felt faint and rushed to call him. "No, Brother, I can't be in charge. I can't do anything by myself. I don't know what to do!" But he was exhausted. I could hear it in his voice. And our team could do no more for us now. I felt as low and as lost as I had since Beirut. What could I do? What should I do?

Shortly after George and Brother had come back sick, a friend introduced me to a Lebanese Druze who said he thought he might be able to help in some way. His name was Nazir Bou Alwan, a small, lean, talkative man who claimed he was the cousin of Walid Jumblatt, the leader of the Druze, who lived in the mountains. He said he would be happy to contact people he knew and see what he could find out. Only a few days later, he called me. His sources had told him that the hostages were now in the Bekaa Valley on the other side of the mountains encircling Beirut, known to be the area where the Hizballah hid, and the hostages had probably been there for months. Nazir told me he was eager to help.

He wanted to return to Lebanon, pave the way for me to come and then send me word when I should.

Although I knew little about him, I had decided it was worth a try. Anything was worth a try. I grasped at a straw and funded him as best as I could. He left with promises he would call soon.

Then just before Labor Day, I finally met with Ted Turner. Toward the end of August, I was talking with my State Department liaison Terry Arnold. "Terry," I said, "it's been seven weeks since you showed me the tape and then projected Jerry's release in just weeks. Surely whatever you were hoping for with the Algerians must be stalemated." Terry agreed, so I asked, "When are you going to show Ted Turner the message addressed directly to him?"

Terry insisted they'd been trying to contact Ted for some time, but Ted was not returning their calls.

"Who's been trying to contact him?" I asked.

"Assistant Secretary of State Murphy," Terry answered.

"You mean Ted Turner's not returning an assistant secretary of state's calls?" I asked. Terry didn't answer.

I decided that I should go to see Ted Turner myself—if I could. So I hurriedly called Ted Kavanau, an old friend of Jerry's at CNN, who immediately got me an appointment to see Ted Turner. I don't know what I thought he would do, but he had to see the tape.

When I arrived, I found out that Ted had gotten the tape just that morning and had already viewed it three times. Our whole interview lasted less than fifteen minutes. He jumped up to kiss me on the cheek when I entered the room. We exchanged stilted pleasantries, and I mentioned that the State Department had said they hadn't been able to reach him all this time.

"Why didn't you call me when it happened?" he said.

"I did. And so did my brother. We were told they didn't know where you were."

Things got more stilted.

Finally he sighed and said, "What do you want *me* to do? People get killed in this business every day."

My throat caught. And then I heard myself say, evenly and loudly, "Jerry-is-not-dead!"

Things went downhill from there.

"Why did you come?" he asked.

"I came to find out what you know, Ted, to tell you what I know and to show you how I think you can help. Maybe there really are more ways to deal with the problem than just the strategy the State Department is using."

He looked at me a moment and said, "What you are saying sounds un-American."

In a handful of seconds, my interview was over. Ultimately, he agreed to study the tape more carefully, and he stood up. He had another appointment. I didn't hear from him again.

From that moment on, I realized that CNN was not going to do any more, or, more truthfully, maybe I realized they could *not* do any more.

I suppose I had harbored a romantic hope that Ted would try some courageous, Rambo-like stunt the way billionaire Ross Perot had done when he funded a rescue of his employees who had been held captive in Iran not long before. I really don't know. Maybe I just wanted to tell him off for the suffocating, silent months. That was possible too. But when George and I left that day, I felt a door close and another one open. Out of sheer frustration, I had flippantly said, "I guess I'll have to try and go get him myself, Ted." Yet the thought lingered. I guess I wasn't through with romantic ideas.

Was it only a romantic idea?

Other thoughts lingered. After seven months of much trial and more error, I was gradually understanding that the next step was my decision and mine alone. I hated the idea of being in charge. Brother's words terrified me. But terrified or not, I was the one with the most to lose. I had to do something.

I had spent all those months waiting, sitting on my hands, being quiet, doing what I was told, hoping and praying the usual channels would work. But all that quietness had bothered me. Something seemed wrong with it from the beginning. I kept thinking how Jerry felt so deeply about the truth and the public's right to know it. The public did not know about this situation largely because I, and no doubt the other hostage families, under a pledge to the State Department, had abetted that silence, trusting that the State Department was doing everything they could. Was that not participating in a lie? Couldn't we be trusted with the truth? There were three Americans captive in Lebanon, probably held by the same people and for the same reason, and our government had yet to admit it or condemn it. And the press allowed the silence to go on, which seemed unusually odd to me considering that what happened to Jerry could happen to any journalist trying to tell the stories around the world. Later, Hodding Carter, the State Department spokesman during the Iranian-hostage crisis, and now a free-lance journalist, would write about the situation: "It's intolerable that the press lets the agenda on a major issue be set completely by the government." And at the end of the year, ABC News' Charles Glass, who ironically would himself be taken hostage in 1987, wrote about the situation in the Committee to Protect Journalists newsletter. In an attempt to involve journalists on Jerry's behalf, he called for "concerned journalists" to speak up by encouraging the Syrians to find Jerry. Such signs, he'd write, "would demonstrate to the Syrians—who are the effective authority in much of Lebanon—that Levin has not been forgotten." But there was no positive response from colleagues.

I had loved CNN's motto: "You Have A Right to Know the Score." But those who knew it weren't talking. Talking publicly, I now knew, was probably my one last hope to raise support to get any positive action at all. I *could* do something no one else would.

And then there was one last thought that also lingered. Ted Turner had voiced it. My suggestion that there might be other ways to handle the situation beyond the government's present way had caused me to be labeled "Un-American." I'm almost sure that was the remark that finally did it. This concept was really frightening. If a philosophy that differs in any way from that of those currently in power is un-American, then God help us.

Why *couldn't* we deal with the Arab countries in a more civilized way? Why *couldn't* we try peaceful dialog and negotiations for a change? What *was* the government's agenda, anyway? More than once over the next few months I would read editorials and hear people in influential positions say, to the effect: "As sad as it is, the hostages have been sacrificed to our vital interests." *What* vital interests, I'd think? Oil? Israel's security? The outcome of a presidential election? How could such things be more vital than the lives of citizens in peril abroad?

All these thoughts simmered and stewed until at the dying end of summer, they finally boiled over.

It was time to go public.

SEPTEMBER 1984

JERRY LOOKS DOWN AT THE remnants of today's dinner—two small, foil, cheese-triangle wrappers and a tin can. Several weeks ago, the guards had taken away his shoes and glasses. Now, without his glasses, he sees only what is nearest him. His rations are still mostly cold, small and infrequent. And he is still losing weight at an alarming rate. He glances down at his hands and arms. They are skinny as twigs.

During the long hours he has spent alone, he has concentrated on remembering faces, any faces. He continues to play the same wonderful scenes with Sis over and over in his head. And by now, he has gone through his opera and football and baseball lists so often that he knows them forward, backward and sideways.

And then yesterday a small, inadvertent gift was given him. He pulls a little wrapper label from his pocket. His guard had left the empty container with his ration of tiny cheese triangles. And on it was a colorful label, a picture of a bucolic scene in the French countryside. Two Guernsey cows are grazing contentedly in a lush, green, rolling, sun-drenched meadow lined with clusters of shady trees.

Over and over, Jerry takes it out to stare at it and savor it, holding it close to his eyes to see every green detail.

A knock and a loud voice interrupt him. Jerry grabs for his blindfold and pulls it on. A guard is entering. Out the bottom edge of his blindfold, he sees the guard's hand placing something before him, just close enough for Jerry to reach. Then the guard leaves.

Jerry lifts his blindfold to see an amazing sight. A book.

And not just any book. It is a well-annotated edition of Romeo and Juliet. *Jerry almost laughs. He picks it up eagerly and, moving his chain out of the way, holds it close to his eyes and begins to read.*

*A Green Line crossing that separates East and West Beirut (above).
An aging grandmother is carried to safety after a day of heavy
bombardment (below).*

Sis, visiting with Syrian college students chaperoned by Sisters of Jesus and Mary (above) and a great-grandmother (below).

Visiting the children's hospital of Damascus (above). Sis always welcomes the opportunity to talk about peace in the Middle East (below).

After Jerry's release, Sis and Jerry make numerous television appearances (above). Jerry demonstrates how he was forced to wear a blindfold in the presence of guards (below).

Back home, Jerry and Sis are greeted by media and friends waving yellow ribbons.

*After stepping off the plane, Jerry addresses a euphoric crowd (above).
But he pauses during his speech to give Sis a kiss (below).*

through dialog. Nobody was doing that now. My conclusions about the situation were my own, molded by my experience in Beirut and then in Washington. Yet my Washington friends were right in one sense. Very soon, I would be termed *un-American, unpatriotic, pro-Arab, anti-Israeli, anti-Semitic* or all of the above more than once.

Jerry's family were also against my speaking out. They sharply disagreed with me, understandably fearing the situation centered around Jerry being Jewish. They were also worried that my focusing on the issues would somehow endanger Israel and suggested I obviously cared very little about its security. And they weren't alone. Many of my American Jewish friends would say the same thing, and it hurt me deeply.

How I longed to explain myself. I was so proud of my Jewish name. And like Jerry, I loved and cared passionately about the security of Israel. But I was convinced that Israel, sponsored by an uncritical U.S., was committing suicide with her current behavior.

Of course, my own family's fears were centered more around how all of this would affect me. But not having Jerry was affecting me enough. For me, going public was like taking steps toward him in an emotional way, so there was no turning back.

I would make for myself only one rule: I would not go on television and "parade" my pain. I had decided early on that the one thing I would not do was cry for sympathy. Too many women in this country have lost their husbands in tragic ways. And abroad, well, in Lebanon alone thousands of husbands have been kidnaped. No, if I was going to ask for support from either those in the West or those in the East, it would have to be because I talked about the issues which brought pain to both.

130

SEPTEMBER-OCTOBER 1984
WASHINGTON, D. C.

After Labor Day, I thought of all the reporters I had turned down back in March as I wondered where to start. I picked up the phone and called "60 Minutes." I chose them as my first attempt to go public because of their huge audience and fine reputation. One of their producers had kept up with Jerry's story, researching it heavily, and they'd stayed in contact with me ever since March 7.

My family was against it. Most were frightened that the State Department was right, that publicity would hurt Jerry. My Washington friends were worried that if I spoke out about the roots of the problems—that talking instead of fighting is what was needed to get solutions—it would be misconstrued as an attempt to get Jerry's release by aligning with the terrorists that were holding him.

Yet I knew that wasn't it at all. I believed strongly that everyone was wrong and the only way back to "right" was

If I were asked to appear on talk shows, I decided that I would hold that line. And in the weeks ahead, as the invitations quickly came in, I kept my rule. When, on the "Today Show," Bryant Gumbel asked "How does it feel?"—just as every other interviewer would—I'd give him my issues answer: "We need to look at the causes of Arab hostility toward us. Instead of cursing the darkness, let's turn on a little light. . . ."

That sort of discussion of the issues produced a flow of letters from all over the world to encourage me. It was amazing. I began keeping a list of the accumulated names of people who had contacted me to offer their help. The list went well over a thousand. In the next few months, the list would grow to include leaders of Mideast nations and the U.S.—Christians, Muslims, Jews and Druze alike.

Then, after only a few weeks, the families of the other hostages began to contact me. And soon we realized we had more things in common than just kidnaped family members. Comparing notes, we learned how the State Department had been handling us all in the same distressing way. First, they told us not to speak out; then they told us not to seek each other, often distorting the truth to keep us apart.

"They told me you had mental problems," Carol Weir, Ben's wife, said after we'd gotten to know each other over the phone while she was still in Beirut.

"They told me you weren't a Christian," I said, and we both could only laugh.

And we all agreed how surprised we were by the lack of governmental support and "hand-holding" we had gotten compared to those families of the Iranian hostage crisis. "Does it have something to do with numbers?" one family member said. Although I hated the thought, maybe it did: 52 versus 3.

The "60 Minutes" interview was first, and I traveled to New York with the highest of hopes about its potential impact. I admired Mike Wallace's no-nonsense, fearless approach and thought it perfect for the situation. They had told me they were going to devote the whole program to the subject. I believed that things would change drastically after the show was aired. I rehearsed and rehearsed what I wanted to say.

We spent hours taping in an elegant suite of rooms. It was Mike, two cameramen, a make-up lady and I.

As we were talking about Jerry, I mentioned to Mike how dedicated Jerry was to the truth, how he would tell the truth even when it hurt.

Mike answered, "Then give me an example of telling the truth when it hurts."

With that, I launched into all I'd planned to say. "There have been no cameras on the hostages, and the public doesn't even know the captor's demands," I said. And I mentioned how Jerry's tape had still not been released to the press. "Maybe we have to learn to talk to all the factions about our desire for a peaceful dialog. . . ." And that is the way the whole taping went. All involved on the set were excited—even Mike, who hugged me afterward.

"Lady," said one of the cameramen, "if I'm ever kidnaped over there, I want you to be my wife and speak like that."

His words were music to my ears. I left feeling higher and calmer than I'd felt since this whole trauma had begun. I knew that this surely would make a difference.

But the show never aired. Months would pass, while I waited and wondered. For reasons I could only guess, "60 Minutes" shelved the taping. To this day, the public has never seen those tapes, just as they've never seen Jerry's.

As I was leaving the set, the producer told me that Ross Perot, the Texas billionaire who'd helped to free employees of his company who had been imprisoned during the Iranian revolution, was on the next set. The producer picked up the phone, and in seconds I was talking to him.

"Didn't they tell you I offered to help you when Jerry was first kidnaped?" he asked brusquely.

"No, I had no idea," wondering who "they" could be.

"Well, what's the whole thing about?"

Quickly, I explained what I'd learned about the demands from the tape of Jerry back in July.

"Look, sweetheart," Perot said. "I'll help you. Call me tomorrow in Dallas, and I'll get my boys on the case."

The month flew by, as I went from show to show, interview to interview, speaking out whenever I got the chance.

Then on September 20, a car loaded with a bomb drove straight through the gates of the American Embassy annex in East Beirut, killing two American Marines and at least twelve Lebanese. George had been right. The *New York Times* ran a story about George's warning, along with the State Department's response that they had not found George's information credible. The nation learned that they had not even bothered to fix the broken latch on the formidable entry gates of the Embassy.

British journalist Jonathan Wright was kidnaped in Lebanon about that time. I'll never forget how I felt when I saw Margaret Thatcher appear on television demanding his release. And I remember being awed only days later when she obviously got it—the Druze militia announced it had found and freed him.

That's also about the time I got a 4:00 A.M. call from one of Jerry's colleagues, Jim Clancy, at CNN's Beirut Bureau.

"Sis, I want to read you an article," he said. Then he read a headline article in the pro-Syrian newspaper *Al Sharq* which reported that Syrian President Hafez Assad had personally become involved in the situation of the hostages. It named Jerry and William Buckley, but omitted Benjamin Weir. The wire services were all picking up on the story, and it was making headlines in Europe. I began to get calls from everywhere, especially from television stations where Jerry had worked. His friends were seeing it on their wires. But the American press coverage was still scant, the story was usually buried in the back of the news sections.

Still, I knew the *Al Sharq* story meant something. It meant I had to go to Syria. I had to go back to the Middle East.

I talked with Carol Weir, still in Beirut, and told her I wanted to go to Damascus, to talk with President Assad, if I could. She said she had visited Damascus herself to no avail, which was discouraging. But she did tell me one more thing. She told me that all her sources there were convinced that the hostages were now in the Bekaa Valley, just as Nazir had told me. Perhaps they'd been there all along, she said. We agreed to talk again as much as possible.

And then on October 26, I picked up the *Washington Post* and read an article reporting a speech that Secretary of State George Shultz had given the night before in a New York synagogue. In it, he said that we should stop terrorist violence by no longer holding back from launching strikes against the strongholds of these terrorists—such as the Bekaa Valley—merely because such strikes might cause some innocent civilian casualties. My phone began ringing— friends and family had heard too. So what could I do? I picked up the phone and called Robert Oakley at the State Department, a career diplomat and head of the State Department's Counter-Terrorism Department. He candidly told me he was horrified by what Shultz said and that any career diplomat would be. Other Washington friends, former ambassadors and diplomats, told me it was only rhetoric or that

Shultz was trying to please the "Israel-right-or-wrong" faction of American Jews by talking of firing on the Palestinian or Shiite guerrilla and terrorist strongholds in the Bekaa. But none of my friends' explanations made me feel much better.

So I asked to see Richard Murphy, Assistant Secretary of State for Middle Eastern and Asian Affairs. Surprisingly, Murphy agreed. When I arrived, I asked him about George Shultz's speech. Weren't they all aware that if the U.S. did bomb the Bekaa Valley, we might be killing the hostages too? After a few seconds he answered, "The hostages are not in the Bekaa Valley."

I didn't know how to respond. So I didn't. I turned to leave, and I heard myself say, "I've got to go back. Some way. I am going to go to Syria."

"Syria can't help, Mrs. Levin," he had said.

Things had been rocky as I went public, but I had thought at least it had been a good move, a move that had helped to awaken people to the continuing plight of the hostages and the complex political problems with which their lives were entwined. Now I didn't know what to think. I tried not to think of bombs landing wherever Jerry was. I tried not to think what other retaliation such bombs would create. I had to go to Syria.

But the U.S. was not friendly with Syria. The government believed that Syria supported its own terrorism, and its relationship with the Soviets was obvious too. Once again, everyone I knew seemed against my going to Syria, but if Assad could help, how could I not go?

That's when a man named Landrum Bolling walked into my life—and Jerry's. Over several months many friends, especially ones at the Church of the Savior in Washington, D.C., kept suggesting I talk to Landrum Bolling, who at that time was president of the Ecumenical Institute, a research and study center operated on the outskirts of Jerusalem by the University of Notre Dame. He was a former college president, a one-time foreign correspondent and editor of a book called *Search for Peace in the Middle East.* I was to find out that this man was known in academic, religious and political circles in various nations around the world. He was respected for his work on behalf of peace and reconciliation, and for the honest and open way he dealt with the most divergent people and beliefs. Silver-haired and distinguished, he is a Quaker, and it was his calm spirit that struck me on first notice.

We were introduced in a little upstairs room at the church, after friends involved in human-rights matters took the liberty of setting the appointment for me. The meeting only lasted fifteen minutes, but he said so much in so little time. He kept saying, "I have a crazy idea"; then he would suggest something that had to do with a leader here and a leader there who could make something happen on behalf of Jerry—or would, at least, give sympathetic advice. He urged that I focus on Syria as a key player in the whole area, especially in the Bekaa Valley, where Syrian troops were nominally in control and where the pro-Iranian Shiites had a power base. He and I had the same hunch that there was something to the rumors that the hostages were being held in the Bekaa. "If that is the case," he said, "Syria is where we should look for help."

Then he mentioned that he'd seen several of my press and TV interviews and that I had an amazing grasp of some of the key problems of the Middle East. It was a wonderful thing to hear. I found myself telling him about my time in Beirut before Jerry's kidnaping, about the children at Mr. Salibi's Cultural Center, about the people I got to know over there, especially some of the outstanding, strong women I met. Perhaps my being a woman also helped me understand more than I realized.

"It seems to me that women, whether Jewish, Christian or Muslim, cut through a lot of the extraneous matter where their loved ones are concerned," I remarked.

He smiled. "When can you leave for Damascus? I'll be in Amman, Jordan, on October 29. It is only a three- or four-hour drive from there to Damascus. We should, of course, try to arrange to see President Assad, though that may not be possible. I have had some private talks with him in the past, but he has had a long, serious illness, and his doctors have made him curtail his work schedule. So don't decide to go in the expectation that we will see President Assad. I am quite confident, however, that we *will* see Foreign Minister Farouk Al Sharaa. I have talked with him on a number of occasions. And also we can see some of the Damascus-based PLO people. They just might have some interesting information and advice."

Without hesitation I told him I would see him in Amman.

And I knew I had turned a corner.

NOVEMBER 1984

IT IS COLD. AND GETTING colder. Jerry has been moved again. The room has no heat. And Jerry is still weak from his occasional, recurring bouts with the intestinal virus.

In this new house, the captors have drilled a hole in the ceiling, lowered a chain and locked Jerry's ankles tightly together. This new way of locking him up is more uncomfortable than before. His sink is a converted toilet, a hole in the floor fed by a rubber hose.

The guards no longer beat him, but occasionally, they talk in their broken English of their causes, their complaints and their intense hatred for America, for its backing of Israel's invasion of Lebanon and for our ships' firing shells at their homes, killing their families. And when they do, Jerry sits silently listening, blindfolded, imagining their faces as they speak.

Shivering, Jerry pulls his knees up close to his body as he lies on his pallet in the fetal position, trying to conserve body heat. He wonders if the guards in the hallway are cold. He wonders if they have a heater. To be this cold is to think of it and it alone. Nothing else matters but to be warm, somehow warm. Yet all he is wearing is one sweatsuit and one pair of socks. And all they have given him are three dirty blankets.

Jerry takes two of the blankets, folds them lengthwise four times and huddles under the layers, trying not to think about the winter to come.

NOVEMBER-DECEMBER 1984
SYRIA

As I made my whirlwind plans to go back to the Middle East, I kept hoping I'd hear from Nazir. His only communication with me since he left was a couple of cryptic calls telling me not to come to the Middle East until he told me to. And that had been weeks ago.

I was going anyway.

Remembering Ross Perot's offer to help, I decided to keep him informed about what I was doing. So I called and told him where I'd be in Syria and why.

I had been getting calls of encouragement from across the country. One of them was from a young Presbyterian political activist minister named Don Wagner, a founder of the Chicago-based Palestinian Human Rights Campaign, who called me every week or so to offer advice and support. So on his next call, I excitedly told him about meeting Landrum and our quick decision to go to Syria. He, like Landrum, had experience in dealing with Arabs, a skill that at that time very few Americans had or cared to have.

For that moment, though, talking to one more American who understood what I was about to do helped tremendously, and people like Don Wagner kept my morale up at very low times. I needed all the encouragement I could get. In quieter moments, I sometimes thought I was crazy. What was I doing, traveling all the way around the globe to try to meet face to face with a president or a foreign minister of a country? But the next thought of Jerry fueled my resolve, crazy or not.

"I have someone I want you to talk to," Don Wagner said during that last call before I left. He set up a time for me to talk to a Middle Eastern woman named Dina who lived in London. We talked several times before I left, and she gave me tips and suggestions on how to approach the Syrians. She seemed well-connected and interested in helping me without any strings attached. It was wonderful to talk to a woman on that level. Then Don rang back. "Did you talk to the Princess?"

"What Princess?"

"Princess Dina?"

Dina was the first wife of Jordan's King Hussein, and I would continue to receive calls from her, even in Syria. Very interesting calls.

So on October 31, I met Landrum in Amman, Jordan. He warned me that we would not know whom we could see or when until we got to Damascus. I remained undiscouraged. We went on to Damascus, where Ambassador William Eagleton treated us royally, providing us with secretarial and translation service and a car and driver. We put all our cards on his table and asked his advice. Although Syria was by no means a favorite nation of the Reagan Administration, Ambassador Eagleton told us our presence could only help matters. "You can go places I can't," he said. And then he offered us any help he could give us, assigning his highly competent D.C.M. (Deputy Chief of Mission) April Glaspi, later to become Ambassador to Iraq, to assist us.

I waited in the Hotel Vendome in Damascus, hoping for the Embassy to confirm that we had the asked-for appointment with President Assad. Day after day there was no word. Back in my room I turned on Landrum's tape recorder, which filled my head and heart with Chopin's First Piano Concerto, conducted by Zubin Mehta. Back in Washington, I had thought it would be a good idea to study Jerry's vast collection of operas and surprise him when he returned. The idea of having plans for when he came back had helped me through those first few weeks. I could never know as much as he does about opera, because he's been an opera buff since childhood, but I wanted to enjoy them with him, anyway. As the months passed, though, I hadn't kept the vow. Now, listening to that music, waiting in my room once more for the phone to ring, I wished I had. So very much. I could suddenly see Jerry listening to one of those hundreds of records of his, belting out the songs, that handsome head of his cocked back. And oh, how I wished I could sing along.

Landrum, though, like time and tide, waited for no man. Under that quiet exterior, he had more energy than a man half his age. By the end of the first day, he had already put out feelers in several directions, concentrating on setting up an appointment with Foreign Minister Farouk Al Sharaa, who was out of the country attending the funeral of Indira Gandhi when we arrived. His office could promise us nothing.

But I did not mind the waiting and the uncertainty in Syria as much as I had in America. Waiting there in that strange hotel in that strange country, I felt a small stirring of hesitant peace. I was in the right place, I was sure. But the movement of the characters was certainly out of my hands. And yet, I think I realized then that it been that way all along. For the first time since the summer, I felt some of the spiritual questions bubbling up again, and Landrum Bolling's presence and hopeful spirit helped me to grow in confidence that there *was* a better way—a studied, honorable way. His attitudes and values had already made an impact on my own spirit. I was daily grateful that Landrum was exactly who he was—a man of uncommon ideas with the will to act on them.

He told me, for instance, at breakfast that first morning that he was planning to ask the Foreign Minister for advice as to how best to go into Lebanon and negotiate personally with the Hizballah, either with or without me—as might be more appropriate.

The next day, though, we were to learn that the Foreign Minister had come and gone without seeing us. And worse, our own Assistant Secretary of State, Richard Murphy, had done the same. But April Glaspi told us that Murphy had made a pitch for our getting an audience. "You must understand," she said, "we can't get in *ourselves*. The Assistant Secretary didn't see him. But we do think you will eventually see the Foreign Minister and through him perhaps Assad."

So we refused to give up. Landrum and I began our "blitz." Many people in Damascus had reminded us how media-conscious Assad was. So they suggested that if Assad had a blitz of telexes from media people, it might get us our interview with him, and then once in, we could try to persuade him of the positive effects of Jerry's release on Arab-American relations.

Before I had left for Damascus, using legal help, I was able to get tapes of several of Jerry's Beirut broadcasts from a reluctant CNN. I wanted to take some of these with me to use as evidence to show the kind of evenhanded journalist Jerry was and to strengthen our case for having him back in circulation to tell the Middle East story fairly and honestly. So we planned to use those to further our pitch for help too.

I called an old journalist friend of Jerry's in Houston, Steve Petrou, and asked for his help in lining up media colleagues to send President Assad telexes at my signal.

Steve promised to enlist all he knew and all they knew too. Don Wagner and Princess Dina were going to co-captain their own media blitz.

After arriving in Damascus, I sent word to Nazir in Lebanon about where we'd be, but I still had not heard from him. We had been in Damascus over a week, and my money was dwindling very quickly. I kept thinking about the thousands of dollars I had given Nazir during the lowest point of the summer. Where was he? What was he doing with my money? Was he doing any good? I phoned Ed Kellermeyer, my old Beirut neighbor. "Nazir?" he laughed. "Oh, that little guy has been by here asking questions lately. Now, Sis, you should know he can't do anything for you."

My heart sank. I didn't want to believe that, not after all the money I'd spent. When I told Ambassador Eagleton's aide April about Nazir and mentioned he called himself a cousin of Walid Jumblatt, the Druze leader, April said she knew Walid Jumblatt.

"Good," I thought. "If Nazir was his cousin, Walid Jumblatt would know where he was." So April sent a message to Jumblatt, asking about Nazir. Jumblatt replied that he did not have a cousin named Nazir. But he knew a little guy named Nazir Bou Alwan, and he was "crazy."

I had spent $10,000 for nothing.

Realizing that I had been taken by Nazir for a big chunk

of our savings, I forced myself to hold back the tears. It had been a while since I had cried. But this news made me think of all the months since Ash Wednesday in Beirut. So many wrong turns! So many costly ones! And now, to lose so much money and the hope that went with it. . . .

I could hear the Muslim call to prayer outside my window and could see the dark clouds which came up this time every day over the mountains between Damascus and Lebanon. They reminded me that just beyond those mountains was the Bekaa Valley—and Jerry. He was only two hours away at the most. The tears came. As the dark descended, the twinkling lights began to pop out all over the mountain, and the stars came into view. As I had done since I was a little girl, I studied the stars as if they held some clue to God's communication. "Just move one little star, God, for me. Just for me," I used to say. Oh, how I wanted to ask the same thing at that moment.

I suddenly felt terribly homesick, but of course, I had no home at the moment. I've had deeply spiritual friends tell of a feeling like this one, in which the longing seemed so deep it almost had to be for a home we consciously know little of. One perhaps in heaven? Maybe. My longing was filled with an overpowering fatigue that no amount of rest would cure. This must be what the word "driven" meant. The only calm center of the moment was Landrum Bolling who was waiting to take me to dinner with Embassy friends wanting to help if in no other way than to give me a quiet evening. Landrum was already overdue for appointments in Jerusalem, and still we hadn't received a message that we would see either the Foreign Minister or President Assad. Could I stay here by myself? Should I?

I looked once again at the stars, and I found myself praying, not in a pleading way this time, but in a quiet way. I wiped my eyes, fixed my make-up and went down to meet Landrum and his friends.

"Come on!" Landrum was calling to me as I came down the steps. "We got a message from the Foreign Minister: 'Come immediately'!"

At 6:15 P.M. we were ushered into the Syrian Foreign Minister's office. Farouk Al Sharaa was in his forties, handsome, well-dressed, soft spoken and seemingly sincere. It would be a preliminary meeting, Landrum had explained to me before we arrived, which meant we would tell him why we were there, and he would listen, take notes and invite us back.

"I remember you and your work," he said to Landrum. Then he asked us to sit down. During the next few minutes, he listened to us, asked the right questions and was extremely deferential to Landrum. I sat there in that richly appointed office, watching and listening to these knowledgeable men talking about ways of dealing with the hostage situation and improving relations between Arabs and the Western world. Landrum's delivery was matter-of-fact as he told Jerry's story, gave the reasons Syria should get involved and explained what an important contribution Syria could make toward understanding and good will in Arab-American relations. I was fascinated.

Then it was over. Although he promised us nothing specific, Sharaa reassured us by smiling and saying, "Let me make my inquiries with the security authorities and with the President. I will be in touch with you again."

When we got into our cab, Landrum was bouncing on the seat with excitement. "This is good! This is really good. Sharaa is an old P.R. man who started out working for the Syrian Airline in London. He can see what we're saying." I couldn't help but feel excited too. After months of silence from my own State Department and Jerry's company, finally it seemed we were being considered seriously. It felt very, very good.

We joined Landrum's friends for dinner. Our host was a woman named Mahat El Khoury, an old friend of Landrum's, with enormous eyes that directed on you the same sort of total concentration that the Foreign Minister's did. I soon found out she had grown up in a prestigious family and had many connections. She was a civic leader, Syrian representative of the Middle East Council of Churches, among many other things, and she was well known for giving dinner parties, often nightly. But during our first few times together, I would underestimate her. She wore many hats, and tonight she was simply a kind hostess.

She had thoughtfully invited an impressive friend named Dr. Sirry Rhoustom, a pediatric surgeon who would translate French, English and Arabic conversation of our small, well-mixed group. He was busy all night. During supper, though, we sat next to each other, and my visit to Syria took another important turn. We began speaking about the Children's Hospital of Damascus, and I told him of my interest and work with the Beirut children in the middle of that war, explaining Dr. Salibi and his Cultural Center. I talked about my interest in music therapy and the plans we'd made to help the children cope emotionally with the war through their cultural arts. I soon found myself going on and on about my conviction that the arts could be an important medium for communication and healing in the middle of war.

For the next several hours, he and I talked about the children of the Middle East's wars. I was enthralled by his accounts of the problem he was having with the children from Beirut sent to Damascus for his care. The problem he was seeing was of the same nature I had been discussing. They were able to aid the children in physical healing, but emotionally, so many grew worse. In Syria as in Beirut, children's emotional wounds were the hardest to heal.

"Some of the children are committing suicide," he said, looking very strained. "Their parents are dead, they feel abandoned, and they are very, very scared."

"Could I visit the hospital, do you think?" I asked.

He looked surprised, then said, "Yes, of course. Sunday?"

Landrum looked at his watch and said, "It's midnight, madame, and your coach is a pumpkin."

I couldn't believe it. I had let four hours go by without a thought of Jerry. A twinge of guilt hit me. Then I realized that I could not remember the last time the dull pain I had first felt last March had let me go. The combination of the Foreign Minister's interest and the charming group at Mahat's party had actually allowed me to forget myself totally for hours on end. It was unbelievably refreshing.

A telex awaited us at the hotel. It was from Nazir. He was finally coming the next day to "report" to us, he said. Landrum could only stay until after the meeting. Then he had to hurry back to Jerusalem to get on with his responsibilities at the Ecumenical Institute. I couldn't ask him to stay any longer. He would be near, and he'd made our position clear to Foreign Minister Sharaa.

At 3:00 A.M., I heard a knock on the door, and I scurried down the hall to join Landrum talking earnestly on the phone to Ross Perot in Dallas. "We've called every day," Perot said. "Didn't you get our messages?"

We hadn't.

"Just let us know if I can help," he said.

Then, just as I was falling asleep again, my daughter Clare called. My mother had developed a malignant tumor on her esophagus. She was to begin X-ray treatments within the week.

"I'll come home," I said firmly.

"No," said Clare. "She insists that you finish your job there and bring Jerry home. Mama, we love you. We all love you and Jerry."

I cut off the light and knew I would probably have to fight with myself to sleep at all—when I heard a light knock on the door. There stood a young Arab waiter from the coffee shop holding a pot of coffee and hot milk.

"We knew you were awake," he said knowingly in halting English. "Please feel better, madam."

The next day, I tried not to think about my mother, about Nazir, about Landrum leaving or even about whether I could stay or not. Being torn between a kidnaped husband and a dying mother was excruciating enough. I could not handle any more at the moment. I would think about these things slowly, discussing them with Landrum over tea. Landrum took me to a nearby sidewalk cafe, and as we were sitting there talking through the *if's* and *maybe's,* a priest appeared in the doorway and strode up to our table. It was Peter Crooks, my British Anglican minister from Beirut. I squealed with joy. We hugged, and then he filled me in on all my Beirut friends. We talked of Jerry and the hostage situation. Peter said that the street talk in Beirut was that Hizballah was picking a "bouquet," the "best of American manhood"—a man of the church, a man of the state, a man of the press, they would say—which surely the West would deal for. I began to hear it more and more after that, as more Westerners, especially Americans, were taken hostage. Then Peter hurried off, promising letters, prayers and the well-wishes of my friends back in Lebanon.

Landrum then told me that he had contacted Druze leader Walid Jumblatt too, and he had told Landrum that "cousin" Nazir was probably harmless but had no connections and could not help us at all. Then he told Landrum that he would relay to Nabih Berri that we were in Syria and that they would both press President Assad to help us. More and more I realized how powerful Syria really was. It seemed everything was checked through Assad.

When the time came to meet Nazir, Landrum told me he wanted a few moments alone with him before I talked to him. I waited in a parlor room outside the hotel's restaurant, as Landrum pulled Nazir out of my hearing and sight. Landrum had decided he would confront Nazir. Landrum wanted to tell Nazir that he should take out his expenses and then return the rest of my money, because we now knew he was conning us. I waited nervously, wondering what would happen. Nazir's reaction, though, was quickly obvious, because after only a few minutes, he came marching around the corner, quivering with rage. He came within a step of me, glared down at me in my chair, and snarled, "Someday, you will have a tall, cool drink and lie on your bed and know what I have done for you!" And then he stalked out.

I shook. Harmless? I wasn't so sure. The word *evil* kept running through my mind. I would never see any of the money back, or hear from him again. All this, and still no Jerry. I excused myself from Landrum and went up to my room. I sat down on the bed and took a deep breath; then I turned my head toward the window. I looked out at the same hills and same stars, toward Beirut. Just over the hill somewhere, Jerry had to be. Must be. I walked over to the window and leaned against the windowsill and stared at the dark outline of the mountain against the sky. "Jerry," I asked quietly, "am I doing the right thing? Is *anything* I'm doing the right thing?"

The next day, after two hard weeks in Damascus with me, meeting with the Foreign Minister and making as many contacts as he knew, Landrum reluctantly let me put him into a car for Amman, Jordan's capital, to make his way to Israel. I took seriously his heartfelt promise to return from "anywhere" if things began to break here. I had decided to stay. Landrum and I had been working on formal letters and position papers to send to Assad if we found a reliable intermediary to deliver them.

Meanwhile Mahat had come up with the perfect place for me to live to cut my expenses. The Sisters of Jesus and Mary supervised a University Residence in the Old City next to the Greek Catholic Church. I would live with the nuns and the schoolgirls boarding there. Those precious women took me into their hearts and their kitchen and kept me afloat for this new and, in some ways, strangest phase yet.

My room was a "nun's cell." It was tiny. It had a small bed with a crucifix over it, a low-slung dresser, a cement floor, no rug and definitely no mirror. Nuns don't spend much time looking at themselves, I found out as I hunted the floors for one. The only less-than-plain thing about by room was a wonderful, leaded triptych-shaped window that opened up over a courtyard.

From the very first morning, I awakened for daily Mass with the nuns. During my first Mass, the sermon was given by a priest from Rhode Island. His interpretation of "praise" was simply that it was not what we *said* to God but rather how we *lived out Christ's life* in us every day. The sisters ganged up on him at breakfast to take my case to the pope. I smiled and demurred.

"Why not?" said Sister Mary, the Mother Superior. "God must have had a purpose in putting you and your story down here among us!"

I marveled again, as I had with my missionary friends in Beirut. These women were so good humored and congenial, focused and assured. They seemed so settled, so thoroughly given over to concerns that seemed larger and more noble than those in most people's lives. Their whole beings were totally God's in a relaxed, natural way—almost like floating, it seemed to me.

I found out quickly that these nuns, though, were anything but otherworldly. It seemed that the Mother Superior happened to know the chief of Syrian security forces, so she began holding secret meetings with him about my situation. I saw her more than once take down the picture of the Pope and put up one of President Assad, winking at me as she was doing it. The nuns also told me they had asked the monastery's "underground" system, their people network who watched after the nuns when they were out helping people across the country, to search for clues of Jerry. From Damascus, Jerry would only be about thirty-five miles away. The Bekaa Valley was that close.

Also on that first Sunday, I visited the Children's Hospital with Dr. Rhoustom. The hospital was a short drive out of town. I was struck by how different it was from Beirut's hospital. Where Beirut's hospital halls were chaotic, full of people hurting and even dying, Syria's hospital was a sort of organized chaos. People were still everywhere, but all seemed to be proceeding in an orderly fashion.

Dr. Rhoustom showed me the way to the children's burn ward. Their problem, as he said, was not enough hands-on affection and care. So many of them were orphans, and that pain was added to the terrible physical pain of their burns. "What these wounded children need is one-on-one nurturing, and we just do not have enough people to go around. In fact, we do not have enough to watch them," he said.

"Watch them?"

"Yes. Our windows do not have screens on them. Too often a nurse will turn her back, and a child will be in such despair, he will jump," he said quietly, looking at the windows. "We need more people."

That's when I knew I could help. I had just found out that a wife of one of the Embassy's officials, Sabine Rankin, actually had a degree from the London School of Music Therapy. And Sister Emmanuelle also had done some studies in it. I knew with their knowledge, we might be able to do something positive here. Maybe the idea of music reminded me of Jerry. He loves his operas so. But there was power in music, of that I was certain, and I was convinced it could help these children if we could just get a program started. Someone once said he didn't care who framed a country's laws, if he could write the country's songs.

Before too long, I was meeting with Sister Emmanuelle, Sister Anne and Sabine, and we were making plans for the children's ward. I began thinking of people I could write in the States who might help. The program had begun.

During that time, I was asked to Thanksgiving services with Ambassador Eagleton and his wife, Kay, and surprisingly, I was asked to say a few words during the service. I found myself talking about the children. I knew we could talk about children when we could not talk about politics.

I didn't know it at the time, but such actions were very important, because I found out I was being watched. Perhaps whoever was watching wanted to know how seriously concerned I was for the Middle East. Perhaps I was a little hard to believe. I would meet people at gatherings and they would say, "I've heard about what you're doing to help Dr. Rhoustom. That is very clever."

All I could answer was, "I did this in Beirut, and I need to be doing these things."

Because it was true. The work for the children, like the evening at Mahat's, was something that could take me out of myself and let me know, in concrete fashion, that somehow, some way I was doing something positive while stuck in a negative situation. At least doing so, I could give something back to the people helping me.

The rest of my time in Syria seemed spent in some sort of crazy Middle East adventure novel.

Quite often, Princess Dina would call me and say, "Sis, there will be a man come to see you. He will say his name is Abdul (the Arab equivalent of Smith). Tell him your story."

Princess Dina had a story of her own, one that paralleled mine in an ironic way. This remarkable woman had spent a year and a half trying to free her second husband, Salah Tamari, a celebrated leader of the PLO who became an Israeli prisoner shortly after the invasion of Lebanon. To do it, she served as a bridge between the PLO and the Israelis in the long negotiations that culminated in the freeing of prisoners from both sides, including her husband. Each time I heard the knock at the door after her call, I thought about what she'd been through, and I knew she was a woman to trust.

And then there were the days that Mahat would pull up to the monastery in a limousine and tell me she wanted to take me to a meeting. So, I would get in the back seat. Mahat would sit in the front and motion to the driver to pull away. Then she would lean back to me and get me talking.

"Why are you here, Sis?"

"Because Syria seems to be the key." I'd say. Then I would talk about Jerry, but I also would talk about my own feelings about the Middle East. And Mahat would nod as I talked.

On the first trip, I remember saying, "It's like my Lebanese friends say, 'I feel my pain is like trying to ease a cocklebur out of a spider web.' It's all intertwined with larger, more complex things I must understand." All the while I'd notice that the driver was moving the rearview mirror back and forth. He seemed to be trying to see me. Yet all I'd ever see of him was his back, his black hair and those black eyes looking back at me through the mirror.

And then we would drive back up to the monastery and stop. The first time, I looked at Mahat, puzzled, and said, "But I thought we were going to a meeting."

"We just had it," Mahat said.

I never found out who the mysterious driver was on those handfuls of "meetings." But with each meeting, I wondered more and more just how influential my new friend Mahat really was.

The rest of my time, between knocks at the door and mysterious limo rides, I'd wait and wait for a call from the Foreign Minister. And when it came, it was always, "Come immediately!" The nuns would never want me to take a bus. They would find money for a cab so as not to waste any time.

"Do you have anything new to tell me?" Sharaa would ask.

Standing alone with Sharaa, I tried not to babble. I would stall for time, going over any information I could think of, information I am sure he already had. But the point of our meetings, in my mind, was not so much to give new information but to keep Jerry's plight on his mind. I had four or five such meetings, and every one was the same. From the start I felt I should discuss Jerry's Jewishness up front. "You Syrians say you don't hate Jews—only the Zionist expansion. Here's a chance to prove it by helping a Jew." He smiled and patted my hand at each meeting. Each time I thought he wanted to say more—but didn't. Two weeks passed this way. I continued to work with the Syrian women on the music-therapy program for the children, but nothing seemed to be happening for Jerry. And even though I fought it, I found myself slipping deeper and deeper into depression.

News had just reached us that another American had been kidnaped in Beirut. Peter Kilburn, a gentle librarian at the American University of Beirut, had literally disappeared sometime during the weekend of December 3. No word had come from anyone as to why he was taken or even how.

Then in early December, during the last weeks of my stay, I sprained an ankle, and if that wasn't bad enough, I became miserably sick, so sick that I fainted in front of the nuns.

During the days they cared for me, I think I recovered not so much due to the medical attention as to these women's hovering care. I have never, before or since, felt so cared for.

And as the days went by, I began feeling that same chemical change I'd felt only a few times since March. I began to watch and study these women closer than ever before, studying this life of theirs, removed from the world but actively involved in it at the same time. Like many other people, I've occasionally found the idea of leaving the world behind for such a life attractive. These women's world was first and foremost a spiritual world, a life centered around God. Death had no terror for them. Suffering didn't push them from God. They used it for him. I couldn't help wondering what life would be like as one of them. There was a sanity here, I decided. They knew something about active patience I have never grasped. And I let them teach me about it as I let them care for me. Nobody, through the whole ordeal, had ever truly been able to offer me hope, but these women offered me a hope based on something I couldn't touch. And through those days spent quietly watching, I felt my heaviness dissolving away.

The virus soon passed, and with it most of my depression. My sprained ankle was going to take a few weeks longer, though. It was almost Christmas time, and I began to think of my mother. I knew I should go home. It was not a hard decision. Maybe it was my illness, but the reality of all that pain, after so much emotional stress, made me worry more about her suffering. I knew I had done all that I could here. Our letters and telexes and tapes were on President Assad's desk, and Sharaa and Mahat had both promised that Assad had said he would help. The music-therapy program for the hospital was well on its way to reality. For now, I had to go home, but I planned to come back. I said my good-bys to the Eagletons and made Kay vow to give Jerry a big kiss for me if she saw him before I did.

With promises of prayers for my mother and Jerry, my nuns packed me in Ambassador Eagleton's limousine to go to the airport. "You'll see him before I do!" I said. "He'll come. And he'll come out this way, you'll see."

"If God wills—*Inshallah,*" I heard someone say.

I thought of the first time I had heard that term. Fahd had used it on the day I'd arrived in Beirut. It was an Arabic term I heard over and over during my days in Lebanon—by Muslim, Christians and Jews alike.

"Yes," I thought. *"Inshallah."*

CHRISTMAS EVE 1984

FOR THE LAST SEVERAL WEEKS—since November—there have been dramatic improvements in Jerry's treatment. At the midday meal, they've begun giving him hot food almost every day. Not enough of it, but hot. And blankets—two more. Jerry quickly folded them to give himself eight more layers to keep out the cold. Then, just as inexplicably, he was given another pair of socks, two more T-shirts, a sweatsuit, long underwear and even a pair of gloves. It took him only seconds to don everything, all the while wondering why they had suddenly begun responding to his complaints.

Yet it isn't enough. Not the food. Not all the extra layers of folded blankets nor all the extra layers of clothing. It is getting colder. And colder. And colder. He is miserable. And he is worried. Easily, he could die from exposure if something did not change, and change quickly.

And now it is almost Christmas. He tried not to think that it could be his last.

The guards would come anytime now for his one trip to the bathroom. Then he would listen to the other knocks and try to picture his comrades—who they are, what they look like, what he might say to them after all these months of silently thinking about them.

The guards come in noisily, giving Jerry just enough time, as usual, to get his dirty blindfold in place. The routine begins as they unlock the ankle chain and lead him to the bathroom.

But today will be different.

When they bring him back to the room, a guard puts a bowl of oranges, grapes, chocolate in his hands. Jerry looks at it all with hungry eyes, holding the wonderful bowl low enough to savor the sight through the bottom of his blindfold. A heart-aching thought of Sis rushes through his mind, and so he asks the familiar question:

"Where is my wife?"

Surprisingly, this time the guard answers. "Your wife went back to America, but she was here a few weeks ago talking about new ways to achieve peace and asking about you in the press."

Jerry is stunned. He is not sure what is happening. He fingers the orange nervously, anxiously, not knowing what to believe.

And then the guard is speaking again. "We want to give you a Christmas gift. What can it be?"

"A Bible—" Jerry blurts.

Two nights later, Jerry is handed a red, pocket-sized New Testament.

"Joyous Noel," he hears a voice behind him say.

CHRISTMAS 1984-
JANUARY 1985
WASHINGTON, D. C.

I was too embarrassed to ask for a wheelchair when I changed planes in Frankfurt, so I limped through the airport and missed my plane home. After several hours, I got the next flight to New York. By the time we landed at JFK Airport, it was Christmas Eve. I hobbled up to the Washington shuttle counter and was told there were no seats left on the last shuttle home.

"Oh, please," I begged, looking, I'm sure, quite pitiful. "This really is an exceptional situation."

"Okay, I'll bite," the agent said. "Why?"

When I told her, she stared at me a moment, then without a word, handed me a pass and waved me into the ticket line. About an hour and a half later, I wearily climbed into a Washington, D.C., cab. "Where to, honey?" the cheerful black woman cab driver called back to me.

"Well, it's like this. . . ." I began. My daughter Clare knew I was coming home, so she had promised to make sure the tenant was finally out of our Cleveland Park house, since his lease had expired. I told the cab driver if Clare had done that, she would have left the key under the mat. "If it's not there," I explained, "then I guess you'll need to drive me back up to Capitol Hill."

"Sure, honey, just a bigger fare for me," she said.

As we rode through Rock Creek Park, I was suddenly telling this cab driver everything—about Jerry, about Syria, about my mother's cancer and my flights back with this ankle. By the time we pulled up to the curb of my little house in Cleveland Park near the highest point in the city, this woman had grown very quiet. Then she hopped out of the car. "You stay there," she ordered. "I'll look under the mat, 'cause, honey, if it ain't there, you're coming home with me!"

It was there. And somehow I got up the stairs. Clare, my wonderful daughter, had even made the bed for me. And I fell straight into it.

I awoke on Christmas morning, glad to be in my own bed in my own quiet room streaming with sunlight. Years ago, Jerry and I had found this house near St. Albans, my church on the grounds of the National Cathedral in Washington. It had been within walking distance to CNN's Washington Bureau, and we'd loved it from the start, especially this room. And as I lay there, staring out our big paneled window, thinking about all that had happened to us since we both lay in this bed together, I felt a chill. I pulled the covers closer to me. I was all alone. It felt so wrong. It was Christmas Day out there somewhere. The Cathedral's bells weren't ringing. I was feeling nothing, though, this Christmas Day. Not for myself, not for Christmas trees and family, not even for the Christ child. I wouldn't be with my family today, since I had missed my flight. Yet I don't remember minding. It seems strange now, but I believe I was given a blessed numbness about the whole day. I called my mother and told her I was fine and would be coming to see her after I rested a little. Then I went back to bed.

Then several days later, before I left Washington to visit my mother, Ross Perot called me with an absolutely astonishing idea. This ultra-conservative Republican billionaire suggested I talk to Jesse Jackson, *the* liberal Democrat.

"He's a sensitive man, Sis," I heard Perot say. "Here is his number. You just ask him to help. Then do exactly what he tells you."

Jesse had been in the news quite a bit during the last year because of his presidential campaign and his daring trip to the Middle East to obtain the release of Lt. Robert Goodman, the American navy pilot who had been shot down over Syria. So I called him. And before I knew what to think, we had made plans to meet. After my visit with my mother, I was to meet him for a private lunch after the press conference at a "Rainbow Coalition" gathering in a church in downtown Washington, D.C. Landrum was home for Christmas, so he agreed to go with me.

We arrived early and took our seats. After waiting through a long series of civic awards and political talks, Landrum motioned me to follow him. We walked right up to Jesse, and he swept us into a side room, along with a small group of his workers.

"We are all held hostage as long as our sister here is suffering," he said to his group. I remembered 'Nsouli's words to the same effect. All of us, then, walked over to the restaurant across the street from the church, and there I asked him, "What can we do?"

Jesse promised to try to pull in all of his Middle East connections and to put his own unique credibility into our pitch for Jerry's release. His approach was like ours, and his frustrations sounded the same too.

"The Jews do not believe that I'm also on their side," he told me. "I'm on the side of peace for all. But too soon there will be a backlash from all of this persecution of the Palestinians. And when it comes, anti-Semitism will have a field day," he said, shaking his head.

For a few minutes we all dived into the authentic soul food Jesse had ordered for us, then he said, "I'm going to London, and I'll see what contacts I can make from there, and if the contacts think it looks good, I'll go on to the Middle East." Then he asked me an unusual question, "Will you gather as many of your family as you can and join me on the platform at St. Charles Barronea Church in Harlem?"

"Why not?" I thought.

The meeting was on New Year's Day, and the media event after the service was an experience. But oh, that service. I have never before in my life heard such singing—and I'm from the South, where black gospel music is a way of life. What I was hearing was spiritual music undeniably bound to spiritual experience. And I knew, like the children of war in Syria and Beirut, we had been offered the therapeutic value of music. And I now felt its healing powers myself. Clare, my son "Brother," and I were in the middle of it. Even Jesse seemed impressed. "You all don't sound like Catholics," he said teasingly to the choir. I remember how soothing it was, sitting there in that warm place, candles glowing, rhythm sweeping over us, pulling us into the spirit of the gathering as we swayed to the sounds of that gospel music, to the feeling of oneness and amazing peace there in that Harlem church.

Jesse went to London after that night, and I waited for his

calls. He met with the Archbishop of Canterbury and his assistant, Terry Waite, who'd had a couple of successes in getting hostages released from other countries through the humanitarian offices of the church. When Jesse told me about this over the phone, I suddenly recalled hearing a sermon by the Archbishop at Washington's cathedral just as I had left for Beirut to be with Jerry. I felt a twinge. I remember being strangely offended. His sermon was about the mistreatment of the Palestinians by the Israelis. It sounded anti-Semitic, some of my friends had said.

When was that? Only a year ago? Just a year?

On January 8, while Jesse was gone, a fifth hostage was taken. Reverend Lawrence Martin Jenco, head of Catholic Relief Services in Lebanon, was kidnaped by the same group holding Jerry.

During his last call to me, Jesse sounded exhausted. He asked me to meet him in Chicago when he returned. There, minus his normal glow, he told me and the other hostage families—who now included the Jencos—that his effort was "premature." He had not been given permission to go on to the Middle East by their governments. "But we could be going fairly soon," he promised us, and the reporters who wrote about his efforts in our behalf. Shortly afterward, he went into the hospital with a collapsed lung.

I remember reading a headline in *USA Today* that said, "Our Forgotten Hostages Wait in Beirut."

Waiting. We were all waiting. "I have not made a friend of time, dear Salim," I thought. I just hoped Jerry had. And I hoped his brother hostages had too. *The Forgotten Hostages.* . . . It was the first time I remember seeing the term, but it would definitely not be the last during the years to come.

Flying home from Chicago, my thoughts wandered back to a day in Damascus after Landrum left. Without any forewarning, I had been invited to have coffee with Syria's chief of protocol at the Foreign Ministry in the same building where I had my meetings with Foreign Minister Sharaa. He told me how Jesse Jackson had come to Syria to do the same thing I was doing, to obtain the release of a "captive." The chief of protocol had arranged the agenda on the last day of Jackson's visit to free Lt. Goodman. Then the protocol officer began to smile widely, almost gleefully at me, as he said, "Reverend Jackson had no idea as we waited outside a closed door whether Lt. Goodman was on the other side or not!"

I didn't really understand, and it showed on my face.

"Did you know?" I remember asking.

His face fell, but only for a second, and he regained his composure. "Of course I knew," he said. Then, patiently, he explained. "That is the point. We chose to help. The initiative was ours. We did not give Goodman back because Jesse Jackson came to visit us. We gave him back because we chose to. We did not give him back because of who Rev. Jackson is, but who we are. Do you understand?"

"Yes," I thought, "now I do. If they want to help, they will. If they could help, they might choose to." Like us, they have their own vital interests to consider. Negotiating with Arabs would have to be very much within their pattern of doing things, often a bit inscrutable and never to be taken for granted. My only solace, as I thought of the event while flying back to Washington, was the real friends I had made in that Arab land. I thought of their faces and felt better.

Jesse had given me the telephone number in New York where I could reach missionary hostage Ben Weir's wife, Carol, who had finally come back to America to consult with their Presbyterian council. We had never met face to face, just talked long and deeply over the phone. Back in Washington, with my ankle propped up on the kitchen table, I impulsively dialed producer Cheryl Wells at "The Today Show" in New York.

"Cheryl, if I can get Ben Weir's wife to come on the show with me, would you want to have us?"

She didn't hesitate. "I'll set it up," she replied. "Call me back when you know whether Mrs. Weir will do it."

So I hurriedly dialed the number Jesse gave me, my heart pounding. When Carol answered, I explained the idea, and she agreed immediately. So without any further conversation, I headed for New York.

My first worry was that we would both have to endure the same inane questions: "How does it feel to be a wife of a hostage?" "How do you feel right now?" If I would have had to answer one more "How do you feel?" question, I was certain I would lose all control and say, "How do you think I feel, you idiot!" But there was nothing to fear. Our interviewer was Connie Chung, and her questions were refreshingly issue-oriented. And Carol was eloquent, speaking with the conviction of one simply telling her own experience.

The hostages' families now were beginning to network in a more earnest way. Even after our first timid contacts back when I went public, it had still taken us all this time to get past the State Department's efforts to keep us apart. Their distortions of the truth had hurt deeply. Psychologists have called such hurt "the second wound." As the science of victimology has developed, certain dynamics have become clear. They've discovered that a victim suffering from "Post Traumatic Stress Syndrome" is often mistreated in ways that are more painful than even the initial blow. Kidnaping is considered by many experts to be the most cruel and painful of all psychological crises. The victim suffers beyond measure, but the family's pain is itself a suffering without visible chains. And it cannot be overlooked. Our particular little group was surprisingly vulnerable in matters pertaining to faith. We were all "believers," even, from what I was told, most of the hostages themselves, except my Jewish-intellectual husband who had always considered himself an atheist. So the attempts to control us by making us question each other's faith, such as their hinting to me that Carol was not the "same type Christian as I was," did strike a chord.

But like most things based on a lie, the control began to slip, and slowly we met and responded to each other. Sharing our faith by praying together was the most important cohesive element we had. More and more we began to gain public attention, and more and more the public began to ask the government the long-delayed questions about what was truly going on with their "never held hostage again" policy.

During those days back in Washington my friend Penne Laingen, whose husband had been held captive in Tehran, had a wonderful idea to help the hostages' families gain moral support as well as exposure. She and Susan Baker, wife of President Reagan's Chief of Staff, Jim Baker, were both Episcopalians just as I was, and they thought we should have an ecumenical prayer service at the National Cathedral. Penne had arranged a service for their group during the Iranian crisis and knew we could do the same for our crisis. But first, I had to get the Bishop of Washington's official permission to hold the service at the National Cathedral. So I made my request through proper channels and waited for the call.

I was in for an unpleasant surprise. When the answer came, it was a no. The Bishop had refused my request. To my astonishment, the reason the Bishop had given for refusing us was that "there are too few of them." His assistant had called with the message.

"Too few of whom?" I thought. We had already lined up

over a thousand for the service. Then it hit me. "Hostages? Too few *hostages!*" I asked.

"Yes," the assistant answered quietly.

"But . . ." I caught my breath. ". . . I don't understand. It was the church that taught me Jesus' parable about going after the one lost sheep. . . ."

Even more quietly he answered, "Mrs. Levin, the Bishop says he doesn't want to set a precedent."

After that I didn't know what to say. I just hung up the phone. For the longest moment, I sat there staring at the phone in disbelief. As I was fighting back the tears, Susan Baker called back.

"Well?" she said.

I told her the story.

"Wait a minute," she said. "We'll just see about this."

In a few minutes, she called back. She had contacted "someone" in the White House who had checked out my story. Her contact told her that the Bishop had asked the White House's permission and been told to kill the prayer service. More and more I was beginning to see that all the manipulation and silent behavior was not my imagination. Public recognition of the hostages' plight was not good for this Administration, and they would do all they could to inhibit any press attention that might arouse public concern, even manipulating the church, if need be.

Susan wanted to tell the press of this absurd rejection when she saw reporters that evening at the National Press Club. But I said no. I hated the idea of squabbling with my church. It had always been my refuge, my security. It was still my church. Such men would not ruin my relationship with it, just as the State Department would not be able to keep the hostages' families from networking.

Days passed; then late in January, a television news company in London, Viz News London, had a startling scoop. A video communication from the captors was left on their doorstep the night before. It was a videotape of William Buckley.

That same afternoon, two of Buckley's friends from the State Department came to my house to talk about what the tape meant. We watched the tape on television. It looked like the one last summer, very homemade and "controlled." Buckley declared, as usual, that he was "alive and well." The term made me shudder. He also declared that his friend "Jeremy Levine" was "alive and well" too. There was no mention of Ben Weir or Father Jenco. He obviously was not being kept in the same room with Jerry or he would have gotten his name straight. Buckley's friends told me they were ready to do whatever it took to get their friend out. Then they told me something quite astonishing—Buckley had told them that if he were ever kidnaped, they should not leave it to the government bureaucracy to help him. They should come themselves. I could tell that they both had been quite frustrated in not being able to do exactly that for their friend.

So we decided that even an anonymous lead was worth pursuing. I called Viz News London, and the man who answered sounded threatened. "News agencies can't get involved in a story," he said quickly. I begged him to let us come to London and talk to him personally. He said he would call me back. Then I telexed Mahat in Syria to tell her about the tape, hoping the information would somehow help. Her answer was puzzling. "All is well for a holiday," she had wired back and told me to keep her message secret! Once again, my friend Mahat was being mysterious, because I had no idea what that message meant.

I decided that I should call and tell Ross Perot about this turn of events. He had told me over and over to keep him abreast of what was happening, so it felt natural to get his input. We had kept in contact all through the fall and winter, but I hadn't talked to him since Jesse's return. So I dialed the number he had given me, and he answered almost immediately.

"William Buckley's friends have some ideas," I told the Texas billionaire. "We're going to go to London and talk to these news people."

Suddenly, Perot erupted. At the mention of London, he said, "I have no intention of paying for anything else!"

"What?" I responded. Quickly, I reminded him that I had never asked for or received any money from him or anyone except my brother, and I didn't understand what he was upset about. "These friends of Buckley's don't expect anyone to pay their way, either," I added. "Is there something wrong?"

"I've had enough of your emotionalism!" he was suddenly shouting. "I had quite the same unpleasant experience with the MIA wives. You're just like them. You're a pushy, emotional woman." And with that, he hung up.

What had just happened?

Was I going to live my life standing and staring, shocked at what kept coming over my phone line? Something *must* have happened between the last time I talked to him and this time. There's no explaining his response. Had the White House talked to him too? Had the State Department? Buckley's friends had heard most of the conversation. They were furious.

"We don't need him," Buckley's friend Chip said.

"We need everybody!" I said, fighting back the tears once again—proving my emotionalism, I suppose—this time in front of two men I barely knew. I got ahold of myself and called Brother and then Landrum. Brother, ever the comforter, told me not to worry about Perot. But Landrum made a quiet call to Texas and then called to tell me that the real problem was that Jesse and his entourage had spent $30,000 on his short trip to London before being turned back—and Perot had paid for the trip. What was going on? Why didn't he tell us he was funding Jesse? Or was it that it would look bad for Perot to be connected to Jackson? Were there more things Perot was involved with that I didn't know about? And even so, why take it out on me at that moment? I had an awful feeling about it all.

Obviously, he'd lumped me into the same camp as the wives of the MIA's of the Vietnam War whose response was not to his liking. Maybe powerful men like Perot had a certain role—a certain quiet and demurring one—that they expected the women around them to play.

In my talks with Carol Weir, we had both noticed a pattern of response from male authorities to us. It was all too often a bit condescending and exasperated. I always felt they thought I was going too far. The subliminal message seemed to be: There was a place for the likes of me, a hostage's wife, and I should stay in that place. Could that be the problem?

The next day, I took all these conflicting ideas to lunch with Terry Arnold, who was still acting as my liaison to the State Department. He occasionally took me to a nice Washington restaurant to help break the monotony of my long days.

I told him about Perot. "Maybe all the publicity around your appearances with Jesse was the problem," he suggested.

"But, Terry," I said, "that was all Perot's idea! He introduced me to Jesse Jackson and told me to do exactly what he said!"

Terry looked astonished. "Perot and Jackson?" I could see him thinking. But he kept his own counsel, as he usually did, ever the cautious government man. I wondered why Terry and I were such good friends. My friends wondered too. He had always played the State Department line, even to the point of trying to keep me away from the other hostages' families. Yet, I understood he had a role to play. He seemed to be able to do it and still be a human being. At least I could always talk to Terry.

"How far is too far, Terry?" I asked.

"The first wrong step is too far in my business," said this expert in counter-terrorism.

I paused a minute, then I looked straight in his eyes. "Do you think I'm a pushy, hysterical woman?"

As might be expected, he was a bit taken back. Both of us started to speak; then we just went silent. I could tell he needed time to answer that one. Finally, he said, "I don't know, Sis. You scare me. You scare us all sometimes. But your heart is good, and the thing is," he said, stopping for a moment, "you get such amazing results." We both laughed, then he added, "Hysterical? No. Definitely not. It was cruel for anyone to picture you that way," he hesitated. "But pushy? Yes. Definitely! My God, Sis, no one can blame you for trying any way you can to save your husband's life!"

I'd asked for it. "I hate pushy people, Terry. I hate thinking I am one." I waved off his look of apology.

Then it occurred to me that for whatever reasons, be they my fault or others', the silence and the innuendo and the failed attempts may have been the very thing that pushed this "pushy" woman into taking more responsibility for what she could do. And then, they pushed her to the press and to Syria.

But whatever others thought about my decisions, I noticed things were changing because of it and would continue to change. Even if the change at that moment was just in me.

So maybe such treatment was good. I could take comfort in that.

"Still, I hate being made out as an adversary of the government," I said to Terry, fingering my coffee cup. To that he couldn't respond. We were opposites in understanding and approach. My new liberal friends and supporters, self-proclaimed "peaceniks" couldn't understand my friendship with Terry or even my growing friendship with William Buckley's colleagues. And I was mystifying my old friends who came from the same background of Bible-belt conservatism as I did. So I found myself stretching between the two. To talk of peace, to be a peacemaker, seemed biblical to me— "blessed are the peacemakers."

In the real world, especially the world of my heritage, the idea seemed to carry a different, almost unpatriotic connotation. I sometimes felt disloyal to my family, my upbringing and my country because I wanted to talk about peace in the Middle East! One of William Buckley's friends said he had felt the same way when he was faced with the reality of being a State Department official at the same time he was friends with a hostage who was embarrassing the government he served. Something about this Middle East experience seemed to hold out chances for everyone to feel maddeningly conflicted.

But we wanted to get back the people we loved. And we knew that would mean conflict.

174

FEBRUARY 13, 1985

JERRY SITS QUIETLY ON HIS pallet, a thousand thoughts rushing through his mind. It has been six weeks since they moved him to this new house. Once again, his room is near the bathroom, and only a few days ago, he heard a new knock.

A new hostage.

On his first visit to the bathroom weeks ago, he had been left alone, and he'd quickly climbed onto the toilet to peek out the small window high above it. What he saw made his heart jump. He was looking down on a town with a highway running through it. Baalbeck! And behind it, unmistakably, was the snow-topped Mount Lebanon. Yes! He knew exactly where he was! If he had the chance to escape, he knew where to go. Straight down that road.

And now—tonight—the chance has come.

The chance.

His heart is racing. Earlier, when he had been brought back from the bathroom, the guard had secured him carelessly. He could get loose. Was it carelessness? Or was it . . . something else?

Those will be questions for later. Much later. Because he has been planning all day. Going over and over each step in his head. Over and over. And now, near midnight, it is time to act. He gets up, moves deliberately to his window and shoves it open. There is a balcony, and he is on the second floor. Yes—it can be done. It can!

Quickly, he ties his blankets together in square knots—not grannies because they slip, the old Boy Scout training reminds him. And even though he has no shoes and no glasses, he does not hesitate. He ties the blanket rope to the balcony's iron railing and lowers himself as quietly as possible to the stony, thorny ground below. And then he begins his shoeless zigzag rush down the mountain, running from shadow to shadow, away from the lights. Dogs begin barking, more dogs and more dogs. Barking, howling, growling louder and louder.

He makes it finally to the bottom of the mountain, to the highway and the city. Then he hears voices coming toward him. He throws himself under a truck.

Lights move toward him, around him and finally on him. Several warning shots are fired, as someone yells an order in Arabic.

Jerry slowly rolls his gaunt body from under the truck, but, refusing to look like a criminal, he does not put his hands in the air. Instead, he puts them out straight in an imploring gesture and says loudly in French, "Aidez-moi!"

Help me.

An armed man moves into his view. He is wearing the red beret of the Syrian army. And as he looks Jerry up and down, the soldier is almost smiling.

FEBRUARY 14, 1985
WASHINGTON, D. C.

Somewhere in the early haze of dawn, around 5:00 A.M., the phone rang on my bedside table. It rang sharply—once. My arm shot out automatically to grab it, and while clearing my throat, I distinctly heard a familiar voice say the most thrilling words I have ever heard. She said simply, "Sis, I think Jerry is free."

I knew unquestionably that it was true that morning, just as I knew unquestionably that he was kidnaped that afternoon eleven and a half months ago. How did I know without proof? I've never been able to explain it. I just knew. The familiar voice was a friend named Kathleen who was dating an old colleague of Jerry's at CNN. He had been called at home when a story came over the Associated Press wire which A.P. had picked up from Agence France Presse, the French wire service. It had said Jerry Levin had been found on a road in the Bekaa Valley by Syrian soldiers. That was all the information they had when they called.

I quickly called Landrum. He called the State Department, but they knew absolutely nothing. Then I called Brother.

"Brother, I believe Jerry is free," I said firmly, but when I heard my own voice say those words I felt the tears begin to flow.

Brother drew in his breath and murmured, "Praise God." I heard him climb out of bed, and then I heard a "clunk" as he dropped to his knees. I did the same, and we prayed a heartfelt, fervent prayer of thanks together. Then Brother asked, "What do we do now?"

The words were no sooner out of his mouth than it began. The call-waiting feature on my phone buzzed another call. I put Brother on hold. After that, there was a continuous stream of call-waiting clicks for hours. As soon as I answered one call, the phone would click, announcing another. And the calls kept coming long after we left to meet Jerry—well into the night, according to the messages on our answering machine. Quickly, I asked Brother to call Jerry's family, and I began taking the calls. By the time the sun was up, there were reporters in our bushes, covering our yard like ants.

At that time, news was very scanty. But reporters told me Jerry was still in Lebanon, probably in Baalbeck.

Did he escape? Or was he allowed to escape? Could that have been what Mahat's mysterious message about the holidays was about? It was Valentine's Day! George and 'Nsouli had told us how important holidays were to the Arabs! Did Mahat know? If that were true, what an amazing frame for our story. He was taken on a symbolic day for penitence and given back on a symbolic day for love.

The next morning, the *Washington Post,* in its story about Jerry, would report that a man speaking in Arabic called the Associated Press in Beirut and said, "We released . . . Levin after many approaches by some brotherly and effective sides. . . ." The *Post* in reporting the reference to "brotherly and effective sides," suggested that pressure may have been exerted by Syria because it was the only steady power that had any authority in central Lebanon.

In a second article, the *Post* quoted a senior U.S. official as saying that there were indeed some indications that Jerry had been allowed to escape and that "there were grounds for thinking Syria had something to do with it." Speculation would abound for weeks, but in my heart I knew he was right. And as the months passed, it became clearer and clearer that that was what had happened.

By the time I was ready to greet the reporters outside, Agence France, which had broken the story from the Bekaa Valley, photofaxed a picture of Jerry, which its Washington Bureau had delivered to me. There he was, long bearded, achingly thin, bleary-eyed and fatigued. And he had scribbled a note, which had been photographed and faxed along with the picture: "Hello, my dearest wife. I am O.K. God willing, I will be with you soon. Give my love to our family."

"Jerry couldn't have been the one who wrote that. . . . He never mentions God," I said out loud. But it was his handwriting. Yes, it was.

I gazed out my window, the photo in my hand, and there were my neighbors decorating my shrubbery and theirs with yards of yellow ribbon. Bruce and Penne Laingen appeared with the flag that had been flying over the Capitol a few hours earlier when the news came. While Bruce draped it across the front of our house, where it would remain for months, Penne, bless her, began cleaning my house.

Before the morning had passed, I had appeared on all three network-television morning shows, along with CNN, and I even met with Jesse Jackson, who was still in the hospital, recuperating. As I returned home, Terry Arnold met me on my lawn, and we squeezed through the herd of reporters and cameras. Clare had arrived, and she was manning the door and by my request had let in only CNN. My grief at their treatment of me was already dissolving in the euphoria of Jerry's return. I was having visions of perhaps comparing notes with CNN, in hopes that whatever we'd done separately could be pulled together, examined and used to help the other hostages. If Syria had helped, then perhaps we could give them the credit they'd earned so that the world could see how it was done, and maybe, just maybe, we could have four more homecomings too—and quickly.

It all made sense at that wonderful moment. I didn't know then that the Iran-Contra affair would soon silence all we'd accomplished and make ours the exception rather than the rule.

As soon as I got back to the house, I dashed up the stairs, ready to throw some clothes together and be on my way to Jerry. After only a step, though, I froze. The other hostages' families! I turned and asked Clare to try to get Carol Weir on the phone. Soon I was speaking to her. "Carol," I promised, "Jerry and I will call you as soon as we can. Would you please call the Jencos for me and tell them the same?"

Although most of the major news networks offered to fly me to meet Jerry in Frankfurt, I readily accepted Terry's offer from the Administration to fly me to Germany on Air Force II. I wanted the healing to start as soon as possible. Jerry would be flown to West Germany by the Turner Company, and after the traditional checkup and debriefing at the Wiesbaden Regional Hospital near the Rhein-Main Air Force Base, we could come home together.

"Whom do you want to go with you?" Terry asked. I knew

that my daughter Clare and my son "Brother" would go with me, invited or not—which of course they were. The rest of our clan would all be waiting here for our return. As Terry waited for my response, I looked around my living room, and I noticed George Malouf sitting on the couch. I said, "George tried very hard to help Jerry, and I think he should be allowed to go with us." George's face lit up. The State Department, though, found some problem with George's visa, and he didn't get to go. I've always felt glad he knew I'd included him. Brother, of course, would go and so would Terry and Landrum. Then I realized I should choose one other. "Terry, I think I should choose someone from Jerry's company." The only person at CNN I'd ever heard from was an indirect connection—Jim Rutledge, the old colleague whose girlfriend, Kathleen, had called with the good news. So I chose him to go with us, and I, of course, wanted Kathleen to come too. Terry said he'd invite both of them.

Before I could even get my hair done, I was flying toward Europe surrounded by the happy faces of those who loved Jerry almost as much as I did.

By that night, we were in Frankfurt, Germany, in a hotel, watching clips on German television of Jerry being interviewed in Damascus where the Syrian soldiers had delivered him to Foreign Minister Sharaa. It was wonderful to see Sharaa ceremoniously present Jerry to Bill and April Glaspi. And when Kay Eagleton later kissed him, just as she had promised, we all cheered. And I was thrilled each time he would hoarsely burst out, "I love my wife. I can't wait to see my wife."

Then in bits and pieces at a news conference in the Foreign Minister's office, Jerry told the story of his months in captivity. We listened in amazement. I struggled to hold back the tears, but most of the time I was unsuccessful.

"I've been in solitary confinement for the whole time, chained to the wall or a radiator or the ceiling. The faces of the Syrian soldiers were the first faces I saw since March 7 of last year. They were good faces," he said, a bit breathlessly. Then he explained how he had tied his blankets together and lowered himself out the apartment building there on a hill above Baalbeck in the Bekaa Valley. Then after walking two hours toward the town below in the dark, he'd heard the voices coming toward him. Thinking they were the kidnapers hunting for him, he had hidden under a truck, where he was discovered—not by the kidnapers but by a Syrian army patrol. The soldiers had turned him over to Syrian intelligence officers in Baalbeck, who had interrogated him and then transported him to the Syrian intelligence headquarters near the Lebanese-Syrian border, then on to Damascus and the Foreign Ministry.

There, visibly overwhelmed, he was told where he was and that he would be turned over to the U.S. Ambassador who would take him to his wife and family in Germany. "That is fantastic," he'd answered in tears. "The Orwellian year of 1984 was not a very good one for me, but 1985 is starting out a lot better."

We thought the day and the night would never end, waiting there in Germany. Finally we were on the Rhein-Main Base tarmac standing in the snow, waiting for Jerry's plane to land. Crazy little emotions surged through my mind. Would he be all right? Would it be the same between us? Then we saw the tiny jet come into sight, touch down on the runway and taxi slowly over to us. Jim Rutledge and Terry Arnold sprang ahead, yelling for us all to hold back and wait until they had "checked things out." I stood on one leg and then the other, smiling my frozen smile. They took forever. Finally, the cockpit door opened, and Terry backed out, leading a dark figure I could barely see through the flying snow. Jim was supporting him from behind. As the cameras all lit up, a hum of excitement surged through the crowd.

I let myself be propelled by the crowd toward this bearded figure with the shining eyes. Then Jerry and I were facing each other, and I heard myself ask timidly, "Remember me?"

He began to kiss my mouth, my frozen nose, my eyes. We clung together for a long enough moment for the world to disappear. It was Jerry, and he was back. And he was wrapped miraculously around me. Then the crowd surged in, and as I watched, my pale, thin, darling husband kissed everyone—men, women and children. And no one seemed to mind. The joy was palpable. The rest of our time on the tarmac is a blur in my mind. The photographs show us happy; everyone hugging and clowning. Jerry looks strained but euphoric with relief. And now that I look back, so was I. Oh, so was I.

Before we knew it, we found ourselves bundled into a car, with a caravan following us to the hospital. "Darling," Jerry said, "I have something to tell you. Something important happened to me. . . ." But what he wanted to say would have to wait. We were at the hospital. They led him off to a hospital room where they were going to conduct his tests and debriefing. I would have to wait in the next room.

Perhaps because he was the first of the "forgotten hostages" to be tested and debriefed, the atmosphere during the days there at the hospital was relaxed. No one seemed to mind when Brother requested to read Jerry's psychological report. He and the head of the department spent hours poring over the tests and charts. He found out that Jerry had scored higher on his tests than anyone who had been processed through the facility. Later, when Jerry would be accused of the Stockholm Syndrome for speaking out for peace and reconciliation, I would remember those tests and know that he was not suffering from anything but a deep empathy for the suffering people of the Middle East—Jews, Arabs and Christians—and an overdose of good common sense.

Finally, after hours and hours away from Jerry, I knocked on the door, opened it and said to the startled doctors and government men, "Enough! You must leave us alone for now. At least for the night!"

They all smiled, and within minutes I had gotten my wish. The hospital staff had rolled another bed into Jerry's hospital room for me. And we closed the door behind us.

For the few precious moments before I knew he would fall asleep, I watched Jerry's face as we talked. A barber had cut his hair and shaved him—all except that wonderful mustache. He looked like my Jerry again. He began telling me the story of his last twenty-four hours, and when he told me how the Syrian soldiers grinned when he came out from under the truck, I said, "Well, it's no wonder they recognized you. I wallpapered their country with your picture." And then he told me that after he had been taken to the Syrian intelligence headquarters, he had tried to lead them back the way he'd come, in hopes they could free the rest of the men. He was sure he could identify the place, but the soldiers who took him back up the mountain did not want to get too close. So all he could do was point in the general direction. The place was at the top of a mountain just outside Sheik Abdullah barracks, which was a headquarters and training base for some of the Iranian-backed Shiite factions. Still, Jerry could not stand the idea he was leaving his brother captives behind.

I had made so many resolutions to tell him all that happened to me slowly, as everyone had advised. But I broke them all and tried to tell Jerry everything at once. As I talked, his eyes closed momentarily, so I quit talking and just watched him, until suddenly he opened them again. He groaned and grabbed his foot. The nurse had spent a long time digging long thorns out of his feet. But she had obviously not gotten them all. I sat with his feet in my lap, feeling for missed thorns with my thumb and then pulling them out.

"How could you run on these huge thorns?" I asked.

He winced. "Believe it or not, my adrenalin was pumping so hard that I didn't feel a thing." He paused. "Darling, the men who were guarding me, they told me you were in Syria. That you were in the papers there. Is that true?"

"It sure is. Landrum and I came to see if President Assad could help. You have to meet the wonderful friends I am convinced helped you."

He was quiet a moment, then asked, "When were you there?"

"What?"

"*Exactly* when were you there?" he repeated.

"Well, I came around the first of November and left on Christmas Eve."

"That makes sense," he mumbled to himself. "Yes, that makes sense! Sis, during that time, I started getting good, well-cooked, hot food almost every day, out of the blue. A potato, chicken, a cup of tea. They even brought me a space heater a couple of times. And more clothes and blankets. And gloves!

"Then on Christmas Eve," he went on, "after I asked about you just as I'd been doing all along, the guard told me you were back over here, talking about peace and looking for me—then he handed me grapes, oranges, Lebanese Christmas cards, a chocolate cake and even a ball-point pen! He wished me a 'Joyous Noel!' " Jerry paused and looked at me quietly. "I don't know exactly what you did, but . . ."

185

I pulled out another thorn. He winced, and then he kissed me. And we sat in silence for a moment.

I started telling him more about the silent treatment I received from CNN and how during those first few months, I never knew what was happening. He grinned. "Well, I for one am glad they didn't talk to you. I might still be in chains."

Then Jerry stopped my thorn hunting and turned me around. "I've got something to tell you," he began again. "On Christmas Eve, that same guard asked me what they could get me for Christmas. You know what I asked for? A Bible."

"A *what?*" I said.

"A Bible."

For the next half hour I sat enthralled as Jerry told me what had happened deep within him during his months of silence and solitary confinement. He would tell the story again and again over the next few years, and it would always be the same. My atheist/agnostic Jewish-intellectual husband had experienced what Landrum later called "Jerry's inward journey." The crucial part of this spiritual journey took place early in his captivity, over a ten-day period. He could even remember the days—April 1-10.

He told me that during the first horrendous weeks, as it sank in that he could be held indefinitely in solitary confinement, he began talking to himself. And that worried him. He thought if he kept it up, he'd go crazy. Even so, he felt a great urge, a compelling need, to talk. But in his lonely isolation, lying hunched on his foam-rubber pallet, his shoulder and back cramped from the constrictions of the short chain, he began to think about himself in relation to the universe, eternity and other humans in ways he'd never thought about seriously. He considered the fact that people had been talking to this thing called God for several thousand years, and they had not gone crazy.

"I thought that maybe I could do that too," he explained, "but I didn't feel I had the right to unless I believed in God. Which I didn't. So I told myself that unless I believed one hundred per cent that there was somebody there to talk to— if even one per cent of me doubted, if even one-millionth of one per cent of me doubted—then I reasoned that I really wouldn't be talking to God at all. I would instead be doing precisely what I was afraid of doing, talking to myself and 'going crazy.' " He called it a "cosmic Catch-22" and not something to fool with.

But as those ten days unfolded, he kept mentally toying with the concepts of ultimate reality, essence of being, purpose of life, fate of humankind . . . the idea of God. Jerry said he felt himself slowly coming closer and closer to his moment of belief. And he was astonished to find that the spiritual package he was on the verge of accepting had to include the Jew called Jesus. Why did it astonish him? Because, as an unbelieving Jew, he had scorned the idea of Christ even more than the idea of God. "Look at the evil his followers had done in his name for thousands of years," he said. And besides, Jerry was convinced that Jesus' prescriptions for peace on earth were obviously unworkable and his teachings on forgiveness were incredibly wimpy and weak-kneed. In fact, it seemed to Jerry that his teachings on forgiveness only served to make the forgiver dangerously vulnerable. He had always been the "eye-for-an-eye, tooth-for-a-tooth" kind of a person. But now Jesus' unique ideas about love and reconciliation and forgiveness were beginning to make sense as he considered his own feelings about his out-of-control situation. What if it's true that we overcome evil with good? And what if forgiveness, not revenge, is the way to deal with those who harm you? What if force is not the final arbiter?

"I came to realize the bully with the gun is the wimp," he

said. "The man who says, 'Go ahead and shoot me' is not."

So Jerry, all alone with all the time in the world to think, kept coming back to this hard choice: Believe in God or not believe in God. Reject Jesus—dismiss him as irrelevant because so many of his followers committed so much evil in his name—or accept him for himself and the potential of his teachings.

As he struggled with this choice, hour after hour, day after day, chained and blindfolded, he kept coming back to those simple, basic teachings. Teachings he knew most Christians did not live by. The more he thought about them, the more they became to him the foundation for the only structure in which genuine peace and justice could exist. There was no justice in his situation. There was no peace in his captors' lives, and their violent ways would not bring any, either. After all, violence would only lead to more counter-violence and where would it all end? So as he pondered the same thoughts over and over in his quiet cell, he began to believe that the failure of people to understand and apply Jesus' teachings in their lives is the primary root of problems the world faces, and acting on those principles might be the only way that humankind could survive.

And with the understanding that came after long days of intense contemplation, Jerry said he approached and then crossed what he called his "spiritual Rubicon," his point of not turning back.

"It was like a diminishing point in time," he explained, gesturing with his hands. "It was a shrinking thousandth, then millionth of a second, on one side of which I did not believe and on the other side I did believe." And at that point, he had prayed his first prayer. He thanked God for the solitude that forced him to think. "Then I prayed for you and the family," he said. "And then I actually prayed for my captors. And more than that, I forgave them as I began to see how bitter they were and how desperate they were. Here I was an obvious pawn in the hands of angry extremists. But it was clear to me that the only way my captivity made eternal sense was that they were actually doing work for God without knowing it. Why else would I, a middle-aged grandfather, be sitting in my underwear in a bare little room in Lebanon chained to a wall? I had to forgive them, because my captivity had forced me to take this spiritual journey of mine. And in forgiving my captors I could proceed, free of the baggage of hate and resentment and fear and revenge."

But he told me it would be months before he was able to put his captivity into the kind of constructive context he needed in order to deal calmly and carefully with the challenge of figuring out how to escape—free of panic and paralyzing anxieties. He was frightened. "You're talking to a mild-mannered Clark Kent—not Superman," he would tell an interviewer. But he was not afraid. There was a difference, he said.

It was only after the strange gift of that Christmas Bible that he came to grasp how, despite chains, locked doors and guards with guns, he was already *free*.

"It hit me like a flash of thunderstruck understanding," he told me. "And, Sis, I knew the next time I had the chance to escape, I would take it, fear or no fear," he said. And that's exactly what happened only hours ago.

Jerry lay back on his pillow, closed his eyes and sighed. But before he dozed off to sleep, he turned his head to me, grabbed my hand and smiled. "Darling, I don't think for one minute that it was an accident that a Christian wife in an Arab state working to free her Jewish husband from Muslim terrorists was able to make a difference. You do realize that, don't you?"

Yes. I was beginning to. I watched as he dozed off to sleep for the night, finally safe and back with me. And I kept watching him for a long time into the night.

We stayed at the hospital two days; then when we all boarded the plane for the flight back home, Jerry slipped silently into a seat with a tabletop and a typewriter, and wrote the speech he would give at Andrews Air Force Base in only a handful of hours, a speech that would forever change our lives. Our lives and careers could go several ways after we touched down in America, I thought. I felt a flood of relief and contentment watching him type, not knowing the plans going on in Jerry's mind. He knew something I did not—it was far from being "over." In his mind, there was only one way our lives could go. He had left men behind, and he was tied to them now in a spiritual way that was stronger than the chains he'd managed to remove. After this clear, internationally televised message, Jerry would never be able to go "back" to the life we'd had before.

When we landed, the crowd full of media and friends and family, all bedecked with yellow ribbons and holding posters and signs welcoming Jerry home, cheered wildly. Then Jerry, after being officially welcomed home by an Assistant Secretary of State, walked to the microphone, and, with his voice cracking with emotion, gave his speech:

"Mr. Secretary, my beautiful faithful family, my revered, precious friends. And you—all my fellow Americans, the most wonderful people on Earth. Boy did I miss you all! But now I'm home, free at last—a born-again American. God has been good to me. He gave me great parents: Abe and Carolyn Levin, who raised me in the greatest of nations with a people and government who value as few as one man's life. And President Reagan's Administration is no exception. I thank the President for all his help in getting me back home.

"Also, while I literally sat in 'darkness and deep gloom,' a prisoner in 'irons and misery,' many officials whom you and I may never know worked long, hard and anonymously to rescue me. And you need to know that while our own government was laboring in my behalf, so were many Syrians. I first experienced their concern for my safety and the safety of the four other Americans (presumably being held along with me) when a Syrian army patrol flushed me out from under a truck where I had been hiding in fear. Despite the fact that in my wild-eyed, dirty, disheveled, pajama-clad, shoeless, identification-paperless state (a highly suspicious capture), I was treated gently, kindly and courteously. I was made to feel immediately that I was safe at last. Then their superiors in Syrian security treated me like a long-lost brother and got me moving toward home quite quickly. I understand this attitude is one that exists from the top down. President Hafez Assad, I am told, has taken a personal interest in this present hostage crisis in terms of wanting it ended safely as quickly as possible.

"Finally God has given me the most beautiful, loving, dedicated woman in the world to be my life's partner—my wife, Sis. I have learned (the past several days) of all her Leonore-like efforts to effect the rescue of her Floristan. King Lemuel said, 'Who can find a wife with strength of character?' I did. And she is 'far more precious to me than jewels.'

"It was written that 'for lack of advice, plans go wrong, but with many counselors they are accomplished.' Sis was helped immeasurably and tirelessly along the way by my dear brother-in-law, Francis Hare; the State Department's indefatigable Terry Arnold; and a man I have just met but whom I feel I have known all my life: the respected and much-loved Landrum Bolling. Finally God provided one of his own to help: the Reverend Jesse Jackson—a fine and compassionate

191

American.

"Mr. Secretary, you are right to say that we must now be concerned with the four other Americans who are still in captivity. They are experiencing twenty-four hours a day, the psalmist's agonizing 'sorrows of the heart.' They must be found. They must be released from the dark pit of despair, the shackles removed from their bodies. But I think we can take heart from the fact that I am still alive and once again a free man. I therefore hope my captors have some human and humane values; and I appeal to them now.

"Let my brothers go! In the name of our common Lord—God and Allah—please let them go! My former captors: I want you to know I am not bitter. I am not angry. But I am glad to be free. Grant freedom to the others now! Quickly!

"I have learned that for the past several months my wife has been pleading publicly for a change in the political climate between our peoples so as to put an end to the violence between us. Although reporters aren't supposed to editorialize (and I am an old reporter), I am going to step out of character and say emphatically, 'I agree with her and pray along with her for a change.' I think we have to find a way to convince people that neither terror nor silence is the solution to the problem. And the whole world must work to stop the use of terror in any case.

"I'm nearly finished; but I want to make this final point that I hope you won't feel is out of order. In the nearly one year of isolation and silence forced upon me, I was able to think and reflect (in a way I had never done before) on some of the deeper levels of my existence and life. Landrum Bolling described the experience to me as an 'inward journey.' It has deepened, and given me a growing religious faith that no other experience in my life was able to motivate. If that was God's reason for putting me in solitary confinement, I thank him. And I thank him for my Jewish parents, my Christian wife and family, and my Muslim friends. The prayers of my friends from all three faiths sustained me through a time I care not to repeat; but under the circumstances—looking back—I do not regret it.

"Thank you."

The crowd had broken into his speech several times to cheer and applaud, but as we finished they grew very quiet. The cameras rolled as Jerry and I grabbed each other's hand and stepped forward to hug as many friends as possible before CNN pushed us into the waiting cars and sped us to their studios for a series of live interviews.

After hours in front of the cameras, the long, wonderful day was almost at an end. The network had booked us into a suite at the glamorous Four Seasons Hotel in Washington. After a happy welcome-home dinner, Jerry finally turned to me and wearily, even tearfully, admitted he had finally given out. It was time to call it a day. We kissed all of our friends and family good night, planning our tomorrows. Because, as of those last several days, those amazing days, we once again had tomorrows we could plan.

BACK HOME 1985

The first few days were not restful, though our friends did all they could to ease us back to normal. Sally Nevius urged us to use their heated pool anytime, but we couldn't because of the media whirl—the network news programs, the "Today Show," a score of interviews with local television stations and off-and-on, around-the-clock interviews with CNN. The most curious, disappointing episode was when President Reagan called Jerry live during one of those broadcasts. As the nation watched, the President seemed to be questioning Jerry's professional judgment, warning him not to say anything that would "even inadvertently, harm those who are still held hostage." Although I could tell he was taken aback, Jerry gracefully replied that the President could count on him and that he hoped he could count on the President to press for a nonviolent approach to solving the problems of the Middle East.

As soon as we were off-camera, Jerry expressed his shocked surprise at Reagan's tone. "Sis, he was trying to shut me up!" he exclaimed. "He doesn't want me to say anything at all. As if a man who was held hostage for eleven-and-a-half months would say anything to hurt his fellow hostages!"

As the Reagan Administration's lack of action for the hostages became more and more apparent, *Newsweek* mentioned the President's "fatherly warning" to Jerry in a cover story on the hostage situation. "He's not my daddy," Jerry had responded.

This was Jerry's first brush with the Administration's attempt to put a lid on the story. And it had started at the top. After that he was no longer surprised to find how successfully the whole business had been kept quiet. As he explained to reporters, by the Administration not revealing the basic facts of the hostage situation, they had "successfully perpetuated a myth that our captivity was a mystery when it clearly was not." One high State Department official told us candidly during that time, "It looks to me like this thing called quiet diplomacy has become a deadly silence." The uninformed public had no idea how serious the situation was.

Jerry was sure that if he didn't help keep the remaining hostages' faces before the public, they would be in danger of continuing to be forgotten.

Mercifully, though, after those first few hectic days of talking with the press, we were whisked off to St. Croix for a month's vacation, courtesy of CNN and the people of St. Croix. This would be topped off with a long sail home via Spain arranged by a new friend, Peter Martin, in which we were guests of the owner of *The Sea Cloud*, a wonderful sailing yacht.

The "honeymoon" didn't last long, though. While we were in the Virgin Islands, we got word that another hostage had

196

been taken—Terry Anderson, the Associated Press Beirut Chief.

Jerry immediately called Anderson's father and the Associated Press, offering to help. And even in St. Croix, Jerry was asked to speak nearly every day. Given the lack of information and public understanding of the Middle East, he felt he couldn't turn anyone down. We were pleasantly surprised to realize the people in St. Croix understood what we were beginning to say. Over and over, during those days, we were encouraged to continue to break the silence. Many residents of the islands, retired Europeans and well-traveled retired Americans, told us it was common knowledge that there were nuclear weapons in the Middle East and that the conflicts were escalating seriously. From their global perspective, many of them told us, they saw the "hostage crisis" as nearly a metaphor for impending war. They understood that terrorism is a symptom, not the disease afflicting the Middle East.

Back home, the speaking invitations came fast and furious. From the beginning Jerry decided we would speak when we were invited. "Whenever asked, we'll go," he said. And that would quickly become the pattern of our lives—big or small, in the order they came, we would accept the invitations and speak. And he would insist we motivate the people we met to ask the hard questions:

"What is the U.S. policy toward the Middle East?"

"What is our position on the Israeli-Palestinian problem, the basis of much of the Arab hostility toward America?"

"What are the causes that lead to terrorism?"

Secretary of State Shultz was quoted as saying it didn't matter what the causes were. But it did, and it still does.

"Terrorists do not terrify," Jerry pointed out. "When President Reagan says they can run but they cannot hide, shouldn't we consider that they have both run and hidden most of the time?" And in a one-liner response to the Reagan Administration's Cowboy-and-Indian mentality, he would quip: "You can't stand tall in the saddle when the horse you're sitting on is standing in quicksand."

From the very first speech, we were concerned about being viewed as "professional hostages." So we were quick to point out that we were only experts in the sense of our own personal experience. And yet as we spoke, we found we were using our experiences as springboards to talking about peace—the power of peace and reconciliation. The more we talked, the more our thoughts crystalized around the true theme of our talks: peacemaking, the most important thing in the world.

"When it comes down to it," Jerry said to one crowd, "if you want war, you get war. But when it's over you don't have peace—only an absence of fighting, which is something else quite different."

But the questions and convictions we so freely discussed before many different kinds of groups—from conventions to talk shows—did not make us altogether popular. It was the same problem I faced when I went public. The idea of questioning the government's wisdom somehow had become an issue of patriotism in the minds of too many people. More and more we saw a rather indifferent press continue to mention the "forgotten hostages" only occasionally, but often enough to inspire a spate of editorials and letters that actually voiced the idea that the hostages perhaps *should* be forgotten. "They knew what they were getting into," more than one person has written.

On one talk show, an "expert" on terrorism appearing with Jerry and me declared that the hostages were traitors for "being there in the first place," even the missionaries.

"*Missionary* traitors?" I asked, shocked.

"Yes, they are working with the enemy," the "expert" replied. "That's treason."

As the hostage crisis dragged into months and then years, we heard more and more of these "experts" being interviewed. Jerry would call them "Washington's newest cottage industry." And many, like the "expert" on the talk show, would hint broadly that any stance showing concern for the people in lands with whom our government did not agree, especially in the Middle East, was traitorous and "un-American."

When asked what Americans should do about the plight of the remaining hostages, Jerry would point to Israel, whom our government supported and whose policies toward terrorism they purported to admire. "We can learn from them," he'd say. "The Israelis put a far greater value on a single citizen than we do, trading thousands of prisoners for one man because they know that what mainly encourages terrorism is the deep-seated, unresolved political differences. Consequently, they take a practical approach to hostage taking."

One newspaper column quoted him as saying, "The Administration is always pointing to Israel as a country that knows how to deal with terrorism—but what we forget is that Israel is a country that has also learned to know when to give and when to take."

No matter what the source, though, I and most of the hostages' families still winced at the "un-American" tag. A neighbor of mine, after listening to me take flack from a call-in listener on a radio show, made an interesting point. She said, "You know, Sis, this is the only country in the world where you can be 'un-'. You never hear anyone called 'un-British' or 'un-French.' "

Of course, just as we anticipated, many tried to write off Jerry's intense call for calm dialog in lieu of loud threats between the powers-that-be as being the lingering effects of the Stockholm Syndrome. Surely he could not want anything but retaliation if he were mentally healthy, his critics seemed to be saying.

This speaking out inevitably had a telltale effect on Jerry's career. After a few weeks, Burt Rheinhart set up a meeting with Jerry to discuss when he would be ready to come back to work. We had talked to Bruce Laingen about that. Bruce had not felt well for a year after his Iran hostage ordeal, and he urged Jerry not to push too hard. David Dodge, of the American University of Beirut, released nine months before Jerry was kidnaped, was still not working. But Jerry and Burt agreed there in my presence that Jerry would take six months' leave to regain his strength.

During that time, we kept speaking, and within two months, in late July, Burt called Jerry and complained about his not being back at work, claiming he did not remember agreeing to the six-month leave. He made it very clear that he did not like the way Jerry was speaking out and "criticizing the President" and felt he should be back on the job before the agreed-to leave was up. Jerry had stood firm with Burt, though, pointing out that he was helping the hostages on his own time.

I remember that I was down in the kitchen, and I heard Jerry's jogging shoes pad down the stairs, so I stuck my head around the door and said, "Well?"

"Burt fired me," he said, his thin face looking dangerously pale. I felt a moment of anger and pain that was on the verge of making me sick. But before I could respond, the phone rang.

It was Burt Rheinhart again. I stood motionless while Jerry heard Burt retract the firing but again insist that Jerry begin work immediately. Jerry again stated that he was being treated unfairly and that he would return the first of November as agreed. Burt reluctantly gave in.

Then, just before returning to work, Jerry was informed that his job would be strictly administrative as long as he felt determined to speak out on the hostage issue, even on his own time. Jerry accepted the demotion calmly. He would tell me that he felt like Moses gazing in the Promised Land every time he passed the newsroom, the operation he once ran, on his way to his desk in "Administrative Services." But we knew then it was only a matter of time before they would fire him for good, if they expected him to keep quiet about this burning desire to help the hostages still in Lebanon.

His commitment to the hostages was costly, yet I have never heard him complain. He'd made a decision, and he knew the price tag. When the remaining men came home we could pick up our own lives and go on, he said. Then he began a tiring two-year effort to enlist other journalists in forming a committee to help Terry Anderson.

Within the next few months, two more hostages were taken: David Jacobsen, the American University's hospital director, on May 28; and Thomas Sutherland, dean of agriculture of the American University of Beirut, on June 9. Both had been forced out of their cars at gunpoint.

As the months passed, others were taken too—people of other nationalities—yet the news services kept on with their same on-again/off-again reporting of the situation. Kidnapings would be reported dutifully—maybe on the front page, maybe not—and then afterward a story on a hostage would only be run if a letter or a videotape from them appeared.

But we were busy keeping the crisis in the public eye as much as we could and pounding away on the issues. Jerry and I were asked to serve on boards of organizations such as The Human Rights Project, Save Lebanon and the Epis-

copal Peace Commission's Middle East Committee. Then we
were appointed Visiting Scholars of the Woodrow Wilson
National Fellowship at Princeton University. As part of the
program, we visit colleges or universities for a week to discuss
with students, faculty and the general public about our experiences.

Then in June, four months after Jerry reached freedom,
two young Lebanese Shiites hijacked TWA Flight 847 on its
way from Rome to Athens with 153 people aboard. And the
TWA hostage crisis was suddenly splashed across our national consciousness, changing everyone's perception of hostage negotiation—perhaps even leading ultimately to the
Reagan Administration's Iran-Contra bungle. And it certainly opened the eyes of the "forgotten hostages' " families.

For several hours that June day, the TWA airplane flew
between Lebanon and Algeria until the weary crew faked an
engine failure and landed in Beirut. Although they first demanded freedom for the prisoners in Kuwait, the Shiites's
main goal was to try to get freedom for 766 Lebanese being
held without charge in Israeli prisons, which they said was
a violation of the Geneva Accord on treatment of prisoners
of war. The hijackers killed an American sailor and merci-
lessly beat other military personnel on board. Eventually,
they released all but the three crew members and the thirty-
six American men. The crew members, including Captain
John Testrake, stayed on board. The thirty-six men were held
in small groups in Beirut.

During the hijacking, right after the murder of Robert Ste-
them, who they discovered was a U.S. Navy diver, one hijacker ran up and down the aisle yelling *"New Jersey, New
Jersey!"*

Captain Testrake wondered, "What has he got against New
Jersey? It's not my favorite place either, but why is this guy

so violent about it?" He quickly learned about the U.S.S. *New Jersey* firing into Lebanon Muslim and Druze areas and that the captors had lost parents and sisters and brothers in the bombardments.

As the crisis wore on, perceptions changed. For the American media and the American viewers, the term *hostage* now had a new face. Hostages weren't just educators and missionaries and journalists, anymore, people who chose to serve in dangerous foreign lands. They were also businessmen and tourists who had no desire to be anywhere near such places.

For seventeen days, the plight of those passengers made headlines. Sometimes the news coverage was minute-by-minute. People across the country would see pictures of the plane and the harried captain hanging out of his cockpit window with a gun cocked by his ear. And the government scrambled to negotiate.

Then the State Department did something that blew the lid off the new hostages' families obedient silence. They actually called the families of the "forgotten hostages" and told them not to suggest that the negotiations should involve *their* family members. These were two separate incidents, they claimed, even though the hijackers' original demand, as with Jerry's captors, had been freedom for the prisoners in Kuwait. It was clear from that that the hijackers were definitely linked to the Hizballah sect that held the men Jerry had left behind in the Bekaa: Jenco, Weir, Anderson, Jacobsen, Sutherland and maybe Kilburn.

For those forgotten hostages' families, the TWA hijacking and that State Department warning were a turning point. The press was knocking at their doors again. Suddenly, they were thrust back into the spotlight, and they saw the power of the media to influence the government's agenda. Peggy Say, Terry Anderson's sister, made an about-face in her thinking.

Until then, she had been outspokenly harsh on those who questioned whether the government was doing anything for her brother and the others.

For a time, her efforts, along with those of the other families, seemed to work. By the end of the second week of the hijacking, Secretary of State Shultz, apparently reacting to the first mass expression of public concern for the forgotten hostages, stated that the government would ask for the release of all the Americans held in Lebanon—not just the ones aboard flight 847.

Things began to look up. The State Department called the hostages' families and told them they expected the forgotten hostages would come out too.

After seventeen long, highly visible days, the TWA hostages were freed. They were bussed into Syria by Red Cross trucks, but the "forgotten hostages" were not among them. Still, Peggy Say was quoted as saying she had learned what the press could do.

After the TWA crisis, Captain Testrake began to speak out too. Of course he was criticized, just as Jerry and I had been, for showing a degree of understanding of the Arab's position, and then he was labeled with the inevitable Stockholm Syndrome. In a long *Christian Science Monitor* article almost two years after the hijacking, he refuted the syndrome's influence on him for two reasons that would hold up in Jerry's experience too.

First, he said, his captors were uneducated and not blessed with brilliant minds. "They really weren't capable of instilling any so-called Stockholm syndrome in their listeners." He believed his reaction came from using his native intelligence and common sense in looking at the situation in which he was stuck and drawing judgments based on those facts. Then second, he pointed out, "a person who has supposedly suffered this impairment should be expected to correct his thinking when he returns to his former environment." In his case, though, he became more and more curious about the whole conflict that caused the hijacking. But his last words were the most potent:

"I think that [former hostages] have a different opinion than most Americans because the majority of Americans, and that includes myself until I was involved in this [hijacking] are largely oblivious to the truth of what's going on, especially in such remote, alien, hard-to-understand areas as the Middle East. So it almost requires us to be involved in those situations to draw our attention to them. . . ."

Captain Testrake had learned what I had. He wrote that there are two sides to the story. "When we focus only on our own grievances," he said, "it ensures that the violence and the terrorism will continue indefinitely." It was sad to think, though, that the only way to understand that tension was to go through such an awful ordeal.

Meanwhile, we wanted to create a vehicle that would keep the crisis before the public and motivate Congress to appoint a task force similar to those which had been formed in other hostage situations.

Two Democratic congressmen—California Congressman Mervin Dymally and Michigan Congressman George Crockett—allowed their aides to help us learn our way around Capitol Hill. Then out of nowhere, a bright student volunteered—Sally Howell, the daughter of a Presbyterian minister—as did Al Staats, a Jewish public-relations specialist. We wrote letters to all the hostage families about a proposed American Hostage Committee and told them we were willing to help them in any way we could be useful, setting a date for all of us to meet in Washington.

Next, we tried, as we had in the past, to meet with the White

House. The word up to then had always been that the President was too busy. Peggy Say complained eloquently on television about his lack of interest, reminding the viewers of the President's unprompted visits with the TWA-hostage-victims' families during the crisis. Responding to the pressure from the American Hostage Committee, he would finally meet with the remaining hostages' families in October, but not before.

To help with our committee's efforts to gain a task force, we decided we'd try lobbying a reticent Congress. And in only a few weeks, several congressmen responded. On July 30, a closed meeting was held, composed of representatives from the White House, Congress and the State Department, to ask questions about the handling of the forgotten-hostage crisis. During the meeting, Congressman Claude Pepper asked Ambassador Robert Oakley, director of the State Department's Office of Counter-Terrorism, why the Administration had not publicly discussed the basic facts they had about the hostages, especially their captors' demands. Oakley answered that since reporters had never pressed them for information, the State Department did not feel obliged to volunteer any.

I remember that I did not recognize the chief representative from the White House who sat quietly in the back of the room. "Who is that?" I asked the person beside me.

"That's Lt. Colonel Oliver North," said Carol Weir. "He's our new liaison with the White House."

SEPTEMBER 1985-PRESENT

After our meeting on Capitol Hill, the press coverage waned again.

But in September, suddenly, mysteriously, the first of the three hostages that would be released—Reverend Benjamin Weir—was freed.

And with his release, the press became interested once again in us. No one at the time knew why he was released, and no statements were given. Months later the National Presbyterian Church would honor Ben Weir by voting him into the church's chief position, Moderator.

Right away, though, Ben began helping us build the American Hostage Committee, feeling as Jerry did about his brother hostages left behind. And as we talked, he told us how the terrorists had moved them almost immediately after the discovery of Jerry's departure. That first afternoon, though, Father Jenco had been put on Jerry's pallet and given the still-knotted blankets Jerry had used to climb down to the ground as his only cover for the freezing night.

By October, the committee's campaign for a full-scale hearing by the House Foreign Affairs Committee had succeeded. But it was not an open hearing, as all the other hearings granted hostage families had been. Congressional confidants told us that powerful members of the Committee did not want our complaints made public. So if there were no open hearings, there would be no press coverage of the families' complaints. Although we went in with hopes high, it was a very short meeting. Before the hostages' families were allowed to speak, Chairman Dante Fascell told them that it was unthinkable to expect the government to make any deals for their loved ones. Then, Carol Weir suggested to the Committee that the U.S. ask Israel to stop bombing the Bekaa Valley since we now knew from Jerry's and Ben's descriptions that the remaining hostages might possibly be there.

What resulted was a stern lecture by Congressmen Tom Lantos, a survivor of the Holocaust, who must have felt that Carol's request was somehow anti-Israeli. He spoke about the brutalization of Jews and monopolized almost the entire allotted time, finally storming out. The meeting was in ruins. And so was the families' morale. We and the congressmen who were interested in helping us set a date to try again.

But that night an editorial appeared in the *New York Post,* branding the Hostage Committee "Friends of the Terrorists." The Jenco family, frightened by the charge, pulled out, convinced it was true. The editorial accused us of being "organized and supported by Arab and PLO lobbyists" who were using the Hostage Committee to help poison the U.S./Israel friendship. To prove its point, the editorial pointed a finger at a foundation of which one of the Committee's key advisors, Landrum Bolling, was a board member.

The editorial stated that the foundation funded pro-PLO publications. Then it called our Jewish P.R. volunteer, Al Staats, pro-PLO and stated that our congressional aides had ties to Palestinian terrorists. The writer of the editorial had discovered that one of the aides was Palestinian, and the other was the widow of a Palestinian guerrilla, information that constituted a terrorist link in the writer's eyes. Al Staats, like many other Jews, had been working for years on behalf of Palestinian human rights. Congressman Dymally took to the floor of Congress and angrily cleared his aide, the Palestinian, of any suggested wrongdoing. Merle Thorpe, president of the Foundation for Middle East Peace, the foundation mentioned, wrote a scathing letter, defending Landrum and pointing out their foundation's grants to Israeli and American-Jewish organizations supportive of Israel were probably ten to twenty times as large as their grants to any Arab or Palestinian groups.

We were all baffled and perplexed, except for Jerry. None of the rest of us knew what we were getting into. We never expected such a cruel distortion of the Hostage Committee's goals and objectives. But Jerry had warned us all along that the more successful the committee was in gaining public and congressional attention, the greater the backlash would be from those who wanted to keep the story quiet. "In the major leagues, they play hardball," Jerry once said, "and that's where we are."

So, despite many gratifying protests against this strange accusation, the damage was bad enough to scare off the Jencos and kill the American Hostage Committee just as it had taken its first steps. And with it died our hopes for a Congressional task force. Jerry was right. Softball, not hardball, is a family game.

Those of us left, though, kept working informally to raise consciousness through media appearances and interviews, and Jerry and I grew very close to all of them, especially to Peggy Say and the Jacobsen sons. I watched as Eric, hostage David Jacobsen's eldest, became increasingly articulate. I saw in his own growing understanding a replay of my own "outward" journey. He told us one afternoon that a State Department official recently had told him if he continued to criticize the government publicly that the State Department would no longer help him try to free his father. "I can't think of anything to call that but blackmail," he'd said, disgustedly.

So we worked to change people's perceptions. Foreign policy, we'd point out, is supposed to be approved by an informed Congress, so we, the people, could have a voice. Not honoring that principle was what swept us into the Vietnam War. And of course, the situation in Lebanon was easy to compare. Most Americans we talked to had no idea that the U.S.S. *New Jersey* was ordered to fire into the hillsides on the pretense of "keeping the peace." But the "peace keepers" killed women and children, and only the people affected were fully aware of that atrocity—that is, until the hostages were taken in retaliation and a TWA hijacker kept screaming, "*New Jersey!*"

At that time, I was speaking often to small groups. One night comes vividly to mind. I was discussing how our mistakes like the *New Jersey* had created Arab retaliation like the suicide bombings that killed our Marines and the kidnapings of so many Americans. In the middle of my explanation, a tense woman stood up and said, "You better not let the parents of those Marines killed there hear you say that."

She had barely finished her sentence when another woman rose to her feet and said, "I am a mother of one of those Marines, and my son was writing me the very things that Sis is telling us before he died."

At an almost identical meeting not too long after that, I was discussing the subject again when once more I was challenged. A young man jumped up and said, "I survived that attack, and she is right." Over and over in our talks, we've heard real people say one thing while our government said another. It keeps happening, even now.

Hostage Peter Kilburn's nieces, Patti and Rosie, told us how during their family briefing with National Security Adviser Robert McFarlane, he had actually told them they had to understand that the "Lebanese raise their children to be terrorists." I almost exploded. I thought of Dr. Salibi crying over his school. I saw all those precious children learning through music about their culture. I thought of Mr. Ghannoum, my Beirut landlord, who would not allow his daughter Hana to come to America with us because he had heard that our number-one crime problem was child abuse.

"Maybe McFarlane meant Iran," Peggy Say mused. "They do say that the Ayatollah sends the children out to sweep the minefields, promising them if they die they will become martyrs and go straight to Paradise."

"That is not Lebanon," I said evenly, not trusting my voice to remain calm.

Months passed, and early in 1986, Mercy Corps International, a relief organization known worldwide for their selfless work, contacted me. I had been speaking as often as I could to women about Middle East problems, because I continued to feel strongly that women bring a very needed dimension to peace. Mercy Corps, interested in these attempts of mine to get women to talk together about peace and justice, told me that if we could get together a well-rounded mix of American women interested in a fact-finding mission to the Middle East, they would fund it. I accepted immediately.

The group, called the Women's Network for Peace, was picked from two hundred applicants and was quite a mix: a CEO of a Seattle broadcasting company, a young Catholic nun who was an anthropologist and a Jewish psychologist well-respected for her work with children.

To help our cause, two of us were photographed with Rosalyn Carter, who had told us she would have loved to go with us except that her Secret Service entourage would not have been appropriate. When one of the reporters asked what her relationship to me was, she turned and said, "Why, Jimmy was trying to help Jerry." In late December 1984, Jimmy Carter, at Landrum's request, called a news conference to challenge President Reagan to be forthcoming about the facts of his hostage crisis. God bless Landrum Bolling and each and every one of his wonderful friends.

We sat and discussed the part women play in peacemaking while the reporters took notes. "Women do not bring the same baggage into peace discussions that men do," Patsy Collins, the CEO member of our party, said.

"That's right," Rosalyn Carter agreed. "Mothers simply do not want to bury their sons anymore." I thought of Ross Perot's remark comparing me to the MIA wives. I actually felt honored by the comparison at the time, and now especially, as I begin to meet MIA wives at my talks.

My growing conviction was that a woman's way is a different way—a voice that should be heard and used as much as humanly possible. I, of course, am not talking about the passivity, the submissive posture, that many men in authority expected of us during the hostage crisis—sitting, quietly watching, waiting, crying softly and reading our Bibles as we remain harmlessly on the sidelines.

What I learned and am still learning is that there is a valuable way to communicate that comes naturally to women, if it is not stifled. It's easier to describe what it is *not* than what it actually *is*. It is not threatening. It is not posturing in Rambo-like revenge rhetoric, nor is it so terrifying that it encourages lying responses. And quite often, it is not a bit faltering in its spiritual strength. During my quest for Jerry's release, I came smashing up against the same male pattern of action and reaction, and except for a few wonderful exceptions like Landrum Bolling, the men responded in reactive ways. It seems awfully late in my life to be realizing what many women have always known: we have a different voice, and we can speak with it. I felt it as I worked with and loved the Lebanese and Palestinian children. I felt it in the nuns who used it to reach out to the world around them. I felt it in my Syrian friend Mahat as she went about her mysterious networking. And I felt it in the women who are not afraid to stand up during my speeches across the country and state their frustration with a world which keeps asking their young men to die.

The voice is not defensive so it doesn't have to lie. It's caring and intuitive, so it doesn't have to threaten. It's confident, because it has learned from experience about pain and about healing. It's the voice of a Southern Christian woman who loved a Yankee Jew and found no contradiction at all in loving and working with Muslim friends to help him. And yes, it's a female voice. I cannot help but believe it can bring something special to the world's hope for peaceful coexistence among different peoples.

At that time, as I began planning for my trip back to the Middle East, I kept thinking about my identical twins, which I guess is also a woman's response. Through all the years of raising those two daughters, so alike in appearance, yet so very different in every other way, I watched them fight over the same turf with genuine rage and then make up. And I

213

thought of the brothers Isaac and Ishmael—the Old Testament forefathers of all the Middle East nations—fighting over the same turf. Isn't the situation the same? They can be reconciled too.

Within a few days, our group was on its way to the Middle East. I wanted desperately for the tour to include Syria. I had to return to thank my friends. But our Syrian visas had not been processed, due to delays. Yet when we arrived in Amman, Jordan, on the eve of our scheduled entry into Syria, I impulsively decided to go anyway. It probably sounded foolhardy to the others, but after my experience in Syria, I felt no fear, no matter what the country's hostility toward America. Patsy bravely decided to come too. Our plan was to try to enter without our visas, hoping we could contact Mahat in time to arrange it on her end.

With our hearts in our throats, we left the other three behind. We boarded a plane to Damascus without any hassle, and I had telexed Mahat for an early evening arrival. Patsy and I soon found ourselves at the first of several checkpoints. I bluffed both of us through the first one by holding up my passport with its outdated Syrian visa. The second checkpoint was going to be a different matter. So I decided to invoke Mahat's name and see where that got us. It got us blank stares from Arabic-speaking officials. No one seemed to speak enough English to understand us.

"Visa?" an official asked.

"Visa?" I replied. "Visa? Where do you buy that?" I said. I thought acting dumb might help. It didn't. "Step aside," he said. We were shuttled off to a room and kept three hours, all the while wondering if this was a very big goof and wishing Mahat would show.

Then they separated Patsy and me.

At that point, I eased out of my chair to look for a phone,

and there came Mahat, arm in arm with Patsy. She had found Patsy in the ladies room. "Mrs. Collins?" she had said, and Patsy sighed with relief. Mahat gave the officials all that they needed—explanations, guarantees of our good conduct and the like—and soon we were tucked into her limousine.

"Do you think, Sis," she asked softly, "that a Syrian woman could get through JFK Airport without a visa?"

I gave Mahat a hug. I had decided that this friend could do anything she had to do. Women do bring something special to peacemaking.

Mahat brought together prominent women from across Damascus to meet with Patsy and me. We asked those women what we as American women could do for them as an act of friendship between our two countries. After a few moments of discussion, the women all agreed that they needed a van with a hydraulic door to transport handicapped children from their homes to the hospital for daily therapy. There were children all across the city who could not get to the hospital for even the most basic follow-up treatment because no one in the whole city had such a van.

"We'll work on getting one for you," Patsy said, as I wrote down *van* on a list I was making of things we would try to raise money for when we returned home. In only a few weeks, with help from Patsy, we sent them that van. After the meeting, we stayed only long enough to see as many of my friends as possible. All of them asked where Jerry was.

It wasn't until 1987 that Jerry and I both were able to visit Syria and thank our friends as a couple. I'll never forget, though, the response we heard over and over. "What took you so long! We've been waiting for you to come back!" so many said to Jerry. It was hard to feel fearful in such a country.

Back with the Mercy Corps group, several days later we

toured all across the Middle East, visiting camps and hospitals, networking with the women of various countries in hopes we as Americans could raise awareness of the pain and need of the country's children and meet whatever needs we could, all in the name of peace and reconciliation.

But while we were there, we heard the latest tragic hostage news. The U.S. had retaliated against Libyan terrorism by bombing Libya.

And in response, the Libyan-sponsored terrorists holding American University librarian Peter Kilburn killed him. We found out that he had been kidnaped and held for ransom by a kidnap-for-profit Lebanese group, the kind I had been told about on the day Jerry was kidnaped. They had demanded millions of dollars for his release from U.S. officials. Then after the failed attempt to kill Qaddafi, the word went out that the Libyan leader offered the same amount to the Hizballah sect to turn over the other hostages in Beirut to him. The Hizballah refused. Then, Kilburn's kidnapers sold him to a pro-Libyan group which promptly murdered him, calling it a reprisal for the Libyan raid.

His body was brought home to the U.S. in a plain wooden box. There was hardly any public notice about its impending arrival. When his body arrived at Andrews Air Force Base on its way to California C.O.D. for burial, news organizations were told that cameras would not be allowed on the base to record the event, which was a reversal of the usual procedure. Jerry called the State Department and was told that it was following "family orders" for privacy. So Jerry called Rosie, one of Peter's nieces, and was told that the State Department was lying. The Kilburn relatives, she said, wanted the publicity. It was clear that the State Department didn't, though. And with his second call to the State Department, the lie was admitted.

The Kilburn family called a press conference to present the truth, but there was little public interest. A collection was taken by No Greater Love, a charitable organization that works to help the hostages' families, and by the National Organization for Victim's Assistance, which asked us and our friends the Laingens to set up a "Hostage Family Project." Between these two groups, a funeral was provided. The Kilburn family was bitter and outspoken. "My uncle's death was an embarrassment to the Administration," a reporter quoted Tim Kilburn as saying. And they were surprised and hurt that the American University of Beirut, for whom their Uncle Peter had worked for many years, did very little to support them during the tragedy. Quiet diplomacy had prevailed again.

Then in July 1986, Father Jenco was released. His return seemed as mysterious as Ben Weir's. Everyone waited, expectantly, hopefully, to see who would come out next: It was David Jacobsen, in November. But with him, a message was sent stating he would be the last one freed.

And that's when the mystery was cleared up. Jenco, Weir and Jacobsen had been part of an Iran-Contra arms deal. The scandal broke.

As it did, Father Jenco publicly announced that if he'd known that his release was bought with arms that would only serve to perpetuate the violence, he would have refused his release. His church awarded him the Pax Christi peace prize for his bold statement. Benjamin Weir, who said virtually the same thing, on the other hand, would receive a letter from President Reagan assuring Ben that no arms were sent for his release. Whatever the actual circumstance was, the drama would unfold slowly over the next few months and years.

When Father Jenco finally met Jerry, he asked him, "Why didn't you come back for me?"

"I tried," Jerry answered. Then Jenco gave him a bear hug. "Jerry, you must teach me about this thing called the media. I've got some things I need to say."

Two men still remained in chains. Terry Anderson and Thomas Sutherland would not be coming out, and before the year was over the hostage crisis would escalate to an alarming degree. On September 9, 1986, Frank Reed, a private-school headmaster in Beirut, was kidnaped. On September 12, Joseph Cicippio, an accountant for the American University of Beirut, was taken. Then on October 22, a writer named Edward Austin Tracy was abducted.

And in the middle of all the fury of new hostages, it was announced that William Buckley was dead. No body was ever released, though. Only a picture that seemed to show him dead. William Buckley's friend, Chip Beck, looked at the picture and said quietly, "Yes, that's him. . . . Poor Bill."

An Islamic Jihad communique stated that they had tried Buckley, found him to be the CIA station chief in Beirut and executed him in retaliation for an Israeli air strike on PLO headquarters in Tunis. Later we would hear from the released hostages that Buckley actually died of pneumonia in their presence months earlier. They said the guards apparently did not realize how seriously ill he was until it was too late and had seemed upset that they couldn't save him.

Then in late November 1986, we would have our first brush with the scandal. The *Washington Post* reported that Ross Perot had attempted large payments to the Hizballah to rescue the American hostages, at the request of Lt. Col. Oliver North. The story said North asked Perot to help after William Buckley was kidnaped. In early 1987, CBS called me and asked me if I ever received money from Perot.

"Absolutely not," I answered. I explained that Mr. Perot had generously funded Jesse Jackson's trip to England to try to reinstate his contacts for the hostages and that I certainly appreciated his gesture, but I neither requested nor received any money from him. The CBS reporter told me that during an interview with Ross Perot, Perot had said that he'd given me money. So the reporter asked if he could come out and do an on-camera story. I readily agreed.

Jerry and I watched the "CBS Evening News" that night. The story about Perot's helping me did not include my reply. Jerry called CBS and asked for the executive producer and the correspondent on the story. The correspondent admitted that he had looked at my denial on the tape and did not believe me, so he didn't use it. Dumbfounded, Jerry asked for a correction. The next day, he called CBS back and asked calmly if there had been any rethinking on the matter. Their answer was yes. They had contacted Perot, who admitted his memory had been faulty. So, that night, Dan Rather read a fairly detailed retraction, reporting that "Mrs. Levin questioned" Perot's statement and that Perot, on second thought, said he had "misspoken."

As the months went by, the country's headlines were increasingly filled with the Iran-Contra affairr. The Iran-Contra congressional hearings were televised, and there was riveting coverage. On July 23, 1987, during his appearance before the Joint Committee, Secretary Shultz was asked by one of the Committee members, "You were not informed that Reverend Weir's release was in any way connected to a shipment of arms to Iran from Israel?"

Secretary Shultz replied, "No, I tended to take the statements of Reverend Weir . . . at face value. . . . People get taken hostage, and then they've been released or probably allowed to escape, as in the case of Mr. Levin. And it's not easy to see exactly why these different things happen."

Hostages were still being taken, seemingly by this same

Hizballah sect. During January 1987, three more hostages were kidnaped: Robert Polhill, an assistant professor of business; Alann Steen, a journalism professor; and Jesse Turner, a visiting mathematics and computer-science teacher, all professors at Beirut University College.

Then during the summer of 1987, Charles Glass, a well-known TV journalist, was taken hostage. Jerry quietly flew to Damascus to speak on Charles's behalf to the Syrian government. He took the very tack that Charles had suggested in print on Jerry's behalf over two years before. In exactly two months, Charles miraculously escaped. Again, most people came to the conclusion that he, like Jerry, was allowed to escape.

In February 1988, U.S. Marine Lt. Colonel William Higgins, a leader of a seventy-five-man observer group attached to the U.N. force, was kidnaped. The Hizballah sect continued to add flowers to their bouquet, year after year.

Still, even while more hostages were being taken, Jerry and I began to see the atmosphere around peace issues change. There was no denying that reality was sinking in, abroad if not at home. In December 1987, the Palestinians opened a new chapter in the fight for their existence. It was called "Intifida," an essentially nonlethal form of resistance. Instead of guerrilla action and terrorism, they switched to civil disobedience: noisy demonstrations, general strikes, refusal to pay taxes, establishing their own alternatives to health and educational institutions set up by the Israelis, and allowing their children to throw rocks at the soldiers occupying their streets. Pictures were taken for the world to see of Israeli troops pointing guns at children . . . and shooting them. It was quite a change. Most Palestinians, including the PLO, stated that their aim was now to be allowed to live side by side with Israel, and to that end they were "shaking off" Israeli occupation. In the years since they began the Intifida, we've seen the opening of dialog between the PLO and the U.S. government, as well as a growing number of contacts between Israelis and representatives of the PLO. Things were changing. We could see it.

In March 1989, we were invited to Columbia University in New York for "The Road to Peace Conference," a landmark meeting distinguished by the fact that members of Israel's parliament and the leaders of the Palestine Liberation Organization sat on the stage and dialogued publicly together in the U.S. "We're all Semites," I can still see Jerry saying with a laugh on that day at Beirut's airport before this whole adventure began.

In a May 1989 speech to the powerful American Israel Public Affairs Committee, President Bush's Secretary of State James Baker encouraged Israel to renounce their "unrealistic vision of a greater Israel" that would take over the Palestinian-inhabited West Bank and Gaza Strip. "Reach out to the Palestinians as neighbors who deserve political rights," he was quoted as saying in a *Washington Post* article.

Among the thoughtful and concerned American Jews reaching out to the Palestinians is our friend Ellen Siegel, the nurse who had been at Sabra camp during the 1982 Maronite massacre. She said something quite amazing. As she spoke of her experience, she finished by making this point: "In 1972, I could count on the fingers of both hands the number of Jews actually involved in the Palestinian cause. Today there exists many strong Israeli and American Jewish voices calling for the right of self-determination for the Palestinians. . . ."

Yes, things were changing.

As the months after his release turned into years, Jerry has never let up, keeping the faith, waiting, always waiting for something to break for his brother hostages' situation. And I have waited along with him. The only lasting effect of Jerry's captivity has been a physical one—a constant, small noise in his ears. They became infected early in his ordeal, and it took several months after he was free for them to heal; the infection took its toll. Doctors told him the noise was there to stay.

We continued to speak whenever asked and to do all we could for the remaining hostages and their families. It was all-consuming. It was, and still is, our life. Jerry went stoically about his full-time administrative position in CNN and returned home at night to throw himself into his work for peace and the men left behind. We became actively involved in projects involving peacemaking, peace keeping and peace education.

One of those activities was an invitation I accepted to go to London to be a part of a presentation given to Prime Minister Margaret Thatcher by a mixture of handicapped and blind Lebanese, Muslim and Christian children. The event was planned to raise awareness for the idea of peace through the country's children—both Christian and Muslim—who could live and play and sing together in peace, and even with respect and love.

While there, I was privileged to visit with the Archbishop of Canterbury, discussing peace initiatives we at home might foster. Then it was on to the children's get-together, which was held at the House of Commons. This peace gesture was the brainchild of an English doctor, Paul Cook, a genius in laser technology, whose work had been used for military purposes. That fact bothered him so much that he decided he wanted to do something for peace. His response was to join with the British Lebanese Society to bring children and adults from both sides of the Lebanese conflict to England

222

to meet together for a holiday.

I brought letters from George and Barbara Bush as well as Jimmy and Rosalyn Carter to offer Margaret Thatcher. And I was thrilled to get to meet her. Even Mickey Mouse was there—big ears and all. We were all introduced over sandwiches of peanut butter and jelly, and punch cups of Kool-Aid; then we were encouraged to mingle.

Some of the children I knew from Mr. Salibi's school, especially the little blind girl with the sweet voice and the pixie expression named Ginwa. All the adults seemed as taken with her as I was, even Mickey. Margaret Thatcher came over to talk with us just as I was giving her a big hug. I can't forget the reporter, though, who came up and asked what Ginwa's *Christian* name was. She didn't know how to answer. She was a Muslim. I tried to explain several times to the reporter that since she was Muslim, she did not have a Christian name, but he looked blankly back at us. And, sadly, I knew that term had a very different meaning to the little girl. The reporter asked again. I could tell Ginwa was beginning to feel afraid, so I wrote her name on a piece of paper for him. The reporter never realized his gaffe.

One moment stands out from that party over the rest for me, though. As I wandered back to the refreshment table, one of the young adult chaperones of the schoolchildren, interns chosen to accompany the children on the long trip, came up to me and asked, "Can we talk?"

"Of course," I said, and we stepped away from the group.

"I'm a Christian from East Beirut," she began. "And this trip, well, it has been a very trying thing for me. You see, Muslims have been lobbing shells every morning over where I live and killing my people. . . ."

I smiled, knowing all too well how she was feeling and added, "And, of course, your militia is lobbing back."

She sighed. "Yes."

"You know," I said, feeling like sighing myself, "we're trying to break the vicious cycle. Nobody really knows who started it all, but maybe we can decide who ends it."

"Well, that's just it," she said. "You see, when we arrived, they put me in a room with another chaperone, a Muslim teacher from West Beirut. I didn't think I could handle it. But you know, I love her. I really do."

I smiled and leaned close. "It's okay to love her. It really is." That moment made my trip worthwhile.

Only a short time later, I received a letter from Mr. Salibi. I have kept in contact with him over the years, continuing to write letters to help the Cultural Center. The postmark on his letter was not Beirut, though, but Arizona. Because of the sudden escalation of the war, he had been forced to abandon the bombed and battered Cultural Center and flee to America. As soon as I could, I began working with many others to honor Mr. Salibi and keep the hope of the wonderful Cultural Center alive so that one day Mr. Salibi himself can reopen its doors and return to his dream of keeping Beirut's culture alive for its children. Also, the inevitable finally happened, about the time I returned from London. CNN fired Jerry.

"It must be a relief, finally," said the man chosen by Burt Rheinhart to deliver the news.

"It's not a relief," Jerry answered. "But it's not unexpected."

Jerry's dream now is to go back to the Middle East in a professional capacity. And knowing my husband, he will get his wish. Until then we're both working hard, speaking and writing daily—keeping that faith. Privately, we've made several trips back to stay knowledgeable and to keep up with our contacts in Lebanon, Israel, the West Bank, Gaza, Jordan,

Syria and Egypt.

And whenever we have the chance, we go to some lookout point on the border and gaze lovingly into Lebanon. Beautiful, tortured Lebanon.

The peace mentality is universal, just as the warring mentality is. As we talk with people across the country, we see them battling in their minds, trying to decide what they truly think about the issues of war and peace and intergroup conflict. And that's wonderful, because it is silence that supports attitudes of hatred and fear and prejudice against those we do not know. In our nation, and perhaps most of the world, the macho military mentality reigns. Might makes right. Force is the only language the other side understands. We can only bargain from a position of superior strength. Negotiation is only appeasement. Yet over the last few years, thousands have told us they don't like these hard-line, hawkist attitudes. Why do they have so much popular appeal? Why do people keep voting for such a mentality? Because people want to feel safe, secure; because they want simple answers; because they have been persuaded that armed strength will settle all problems and guarantee peace and security.

Yet a retired Israeli general, Hakarbi, a hero of the 1967 Six Day War, has said that Israel's military might is not where their security must be found. "It's very urgent that we negotiate peace with our Arab nations—now," he said at a recent meeting where I heard him speak. Here is a man who personally helped to build the strongest military force in the Middle East (backed by American money), and he still comes down on the side of negotiation—even while so many of his governmental officials continue to chafe at the idea. To our amazement, representatives of Israeli intelligence, perhaps a new guard of younger and wiser persons, recently made news by expressing much the same sentiment to their government. More than once during these years, I've been told that the strife in all the Middle East stems from the Israeli-Arab conflict. Nothing else can *begin* to be settled until this issue is resolved.

I've gone back to graduate school, turning from theology to Peace Studies, to fine-tune my teaching skills. And as I read and ponder such topics as historic conflict resolution, I marvel at the manipulation of our Western public opinion by a handful of people. I find it fascinating because it is all so real to me as I actually see how such history fits into my own life. But even though I know that such manipulation is still so real and so insidious, I believe it's possible to be heard from the grassroots. And that is the one overriding reason that Jerry and I continue to speak whenever we're asked.

Today, Jerry and I are at Notre Dame University. We are in a classroom of bright students, an ethics class, and it is question-and-answer time. The subject of the discussion involves U.S. aid to Israel and the Israeli treatment of the Palestinians, and it is heating up.

"We have a promise to keep with Israel. They deserve a homeland," one is saying.

"But don't Palestinians deserve a homeland too? Are we a moral people if we ignore one for the sake of the other?" says another.

The students are debating among themselves, and they are bouncing it back to us. Listening closely, I am enthralled and heartened. I glance at Jerry, and he is smiling too. Talk, discussion, calm debate. This is the key.

Suddenly, as the voices swirl around me, I think of Beirut. I see myself on those first innocent days, before our lives did their respective backflips, in Fahd's car with Jerry, flying down the streets on the way from the airport.

"Maybe I'll become an expert on the Middle East," I had

smiled and said, so casually, as Fahd dodged piles of debris. And I see Fahd frown, lean back, his plastic Ayatollah picture swaying, and say, "You do not have enough time."

As I listen to the students, I shake my head ever so slightly at the memory—and at myself.

How much I've learned since that moment; how much I still have to learn. How much more we all should be trying to learn. If there is time.

MAJOR CHARACTERS, PLACES, TERMS

Lebanon

Amal: "Hope." The major Shiite Muslim Lebanese political faction and militia. Led by Nabih Berri, Amal wants to reform Lebanon's political institutions to give Shiites a greater say in running the country.

Bekaa Valley: Long valley in eastern Lebanon lined by mountains. It is the site of a number of Iranian-backed radical strongholds.

Baalbeck: Main Bekaa Valley city, a center of radical Iranian-backed revolutionary activity and headquarters of a 2,000-man Iranian military force known as the Revolutionary Guards.

Nabih Berri: Leader of the still-dominant Lebanese Shiite faction, Amal, meaning "Hope." Unlike Hizballah, Amal's aim has not been to overthrow the nation's political institutions but instead push for reforms that would give the Shiite community greater political leverage. It is closely aligned with Syria.

Druze: Small but historically powerful Lebanese sect living mainly in the mountains of Lebanon, neighboring Syria and Israel. Their secretive religion, probably an offshoot of Islam, is closed to outsiders, and some of its elements are only known by its leaders.

Sheik Mohammed Hussein Fadlallah: A leading Lebanese Shiite spiritual leader. Admittedly one of the main spiritual leaders of the Hizballah.

Amin Gemayel: Maronite Christian president of Lebanon from 1982-1988. He was elected to office to replace his Phalangist strong-man brother who had been assassinated a few days before he was to become President. By the last day of Amin Gemayel's six-year term, Lebanon's deadlocked and intimidated Parliament had not elected a successor, leaving two governments in place: one led by Sunni Prime Minister Selim Hoss, and the other led by General Michel Aoun, the Maronite Commander of the Lebanese Army, whom Gemayael appointed at the eleventh hour to try to run the country.

Hizballah: "Party of God." Radical Iranian-backed Lebanese Shiite faction that wants to revolutionize Lebanon's political system and replace it with an Iranian-style Islamic government.

Walid Jumblatt: Social and political leader of a majority of Lebanon's Druze. The name of his political organization is the PSP (Progressive Socialist Party), which also fields one of the stronger militias. Like Amal, it is closely tied to Syria.

Ayatollah Ruhollah Khomeini: Late spiritual leader of Islam's Shiites and also leader of the Iranian revolution that replaced the late Shah's authoritarian monarchy with an equally authoritarian Islamic regime under considerable control of the nation's religious hierarchy.

Maronite Catholics: One of the most powerful Christian sects in Lebanon. In keeping with a verbal agreement made nearly over forty years ago, the President of Lebanon and the head of the armed forces has been a Maronite, while the Prime Minister has been a Sunni Muslim and the Speaker of the Parliament a Shiite Muslim.

Phalange: Political and military arm of Lebanon's Maronite Christian sect, founded in the 1930s by Amin Gemayel's father. Lately the Phalange has absorbed other less powerful Christian militias and has been calling this new, combined paramilitary machine *the Lebanese Forces.*

Sabra and Shatilla: Two West Beirut Palestinian refugee camps. Scene of the last massacre of defenseless Palestinian men, women and children in the refugee camps by the Phalange. In this last instance (September 1982) the massacre took place while Israeli troops stood by. Ironically in later years Palestinians were to die violent deaths again in those same camps and in even greater numbers, but this time because of deadly Amal sieges and bombardments.

Ghassan Siblani: In the mid-1980s he was a member of Nabih Berri's inner circle, often its spokesman. Sometimes he was referred to as Berri's right-hand man, although it is not certain if he actually wielded that much power.

Shiite: Follower of one of the major branches of Islam, who claim that true Muslim leadership descended through Ali, the son-in-law of the Prophet Muhammad. As much as twenty per cent of the Muslim world may be Shiite. The majority of Iranian and Lebanese Muslims are Shiite.

Sunni: Majority branch of Islam. But in Lebanon they have become the minority Muslim sect. Historically they have been better off economically and socially, and stronger politically than Lebanon's Shiite Muslims.

Beirut
CNN: Cable News Network, Jerry's company

Violet Copti: Palestinian Arabic teacher

Joan Crooks: British missionary

Peter Crooks: British chaplain

Fahd: CNN Lebanese driver

Hana Ghannoum: Eldest daughter of Sis and Jerry's landlord

Mr. Ghannoum: Sis and Jerry's landlord

Ed Kellermeyer: American businessman, Sis and Jerry's apartment neighbor

Donald Marston: Former British Embassy officer

Sami Salibi: Director of Cultural Center

Salim: CNN Lebanese driver

Ed Turner: CNN number-two man

USA
Nazir Bou Alwan: Lebanese Druze sent to Lebanon by Sis

Elizabeth Aldridge: Washington, D.C., friend and confidant

Terry Arnold: State Department officer, Department of Counter Terrorism. Sis's final liaison officer

Landrum Bolling: Widely respected peace advocate, scholar, college president, who went to Syria with Sis

Francis "Brother" Hare, Jr.: Sis's brother

Sue Hare: Brother's wife

Jesse Jackson: American religious leader, civil rights activist and politician. Made effort to free Jerry through diplomatic channels

Bruce Laingen: Highest-ranking American diplomat held during Iranian hostage crisis of 1979-1980

Penne Laingen: Longtime friend and college classmate of Sis. Wife of Bruce Laingen

George Malouf: Lebanese businessman, part of "team"

Sally and Jack Nevius: Sis and Jerry's closest friends in Washington, D.C.

Munir 'Nsouli: Former Lebanese ambassador, part of "team"

Robert Oakley: State Department officer, head of Counter-Terrorism Department during first years of hostage crisis

Jay Parker: Long-time friend of Sis and Jerry. A Washington attorney, part of "team"

Ross Perot: Texas billionaire who financed Jackson's effort

Burt Rheinhart: President of CNN

Ted Turner: Founder/chairman of CNN and Turner Broadcasting Company

Damascus
Hafez Assad: President of Syria

Princess Dina: Egyptian ex-wife of Jordan's King Hussein. Popular Arab heroine of Israeli-Palestinian conflict

William Eagleton: U.S. Ambassador to Syria while Jerry was in captivity

Kay Eagleton: Wife of Ambassador Eagleton

April Glaspi: Ambassador Eagleton's Deputy Chief of Mission

Mahat El Khourey: Landrum Bolling's well-connected Syrian friend

Farouk al Sharaa: Syrian Foreign Minister

Sisters of Jesus and Mary: Mary, Helen, Emmanuelle, Lourdes, Mary Therese, Bridget, who befriended Sis in Syria

Hostages and Families

Terry Anderson: Associated Press Bureau Chief, kidnaped March 16, 1985

William Buckley: U.S. Embassy Officer-CIA, kidnaped March 16, 1984

William Higgins: U.S. Marine Colonel, kidnaped, February 17, 1988

David Jacobsen: Hospital director of American University of Beirut, kidnaped May 28, 1985

Father Lawrence Martin Jenco: Head of Catholic Relief Services, kidnaped January 8, 1985

Peter Kilburn: Librarian at American University of Beirut, disappeared December 3, 1984

Robert Polhill: Assistant professor of business, Beirut University College, kidnaped January 24, 1987

Peggy Say: Sister of hostage Terry Anderson

Alann Steen: Journalism professor, Beirut University College, kidnaped January 24, 1987

Thomas Sutherland: Dean of agriculture, American University of Beirut, kidnaped June 9, 1985

Jesse Turner: Visiting mathematics and computer science professor, Beirut University College, kidnaped January 24, 1987

Benjamin Weir: Presbyterian missionary, kidnaped May 8, 1984

Carol Weir: Benjamin Weir's wife

CHRONOLOGY OF EVENTS

1982
June 6: Israel invades Lebanon.

July 21: David Dodge, acting president of the American University of Beirut, is kidnaped.

August 18: United States, Britain, France and Italy form a multi-national "peace-keeping force" to supervise the evacuation of the PLO from Beirut.

September 16-18: The Maronite Christian Phalange militia massacre of several hundred Palestinian civilians at Sabra and Shatilla refugee camps, while Israeli troops stand by.

1983
April 18: U.S. Embassy in West Beirut is destroyed, with considerable loss of life, by car bomb. The Islamic Jihad claims credit.

July 23: David Dodge is released from captivity exactly one year to the day after he was taken hostage. Syria helps gain his release.

September 19-22: U.S. Special Envoy Robert McFarlane successfully urges the abandonment of the U.S. peace-keeping force's neutrality. Offshore naval guns are ordered to fire on Lebanese Druze, Muslim and Syrian oppositions.

October 23: In retaliation, two coordinated, early-morning suicide car bombings result in the deaths of 241 U.S. Marines stationed at Beirut's International Airport and also 58 French paratroopers stationed further downtown.

December 4: Two U.S. Navy fighter planes are shot down over Lebanon by Syrian gunners. One pilot dies; the other, Lt. Robert Goodman, is taken prisoner. The battleship U.S.S. *New Jersey* starts shelling the Shouf mountains overlooking Beirut.

December 23: Jerry Levin arrives in Beirut.

December 30: He reports Islamic Jihad's end-of-year threat to make "the earth tremble beneath the feet of America in 1984."

1984
January 2: Syria releases Lt. Goodman to Jesse Jackson.

January 18: Malcolm Kerr, American University of Beirut president, is assassinated.

January 22: Sis Levin arrives in Beirut.

February 6: Siege of West Beirut. Muslim and Druze militias take control.

February 10: Frank Regier, American University of Beirut professor, is kidnaped.

February 27: Jerry covers the withdrawal of the U.S. Marines from Beirut.

March 7: Jerry is kidnaped.

March 16: William Buckley, U.S. Embassy political officer (and CIA station chief), is kidnaped.

March 16: Sis leaves for Cyprus and ultimately the U.S.

April 15: Shiite Muslim Amal militia raid on West Beirut house to free Jerry instead frees two other hostages: American University of Beirut professor Frank Regier and French businessman Christian Joubert.

May 8: Presbyterian missionary Benjamin Weir is kidnaped.

July 5: Jerry is videotaped reading statement prepared by his captors. It demands freedom for imprisoned terrorists in Kuwait in return for his freedom. The other hostages are required to record similar statements. Sis is shown the videotape a week later in Washington, D.C.

Late August: Sis decides to go public.

September 20: American Embassy in East Beirut is bombed after warning provided by Sis's investigator, George Malouf, goes unheeded.

October 31: Sis and Landrum Bolling travel to Damascus to appeal for Syrian help.

December 3: Peter Kilburn, American University of Beirut librarian, disappears in Beirut. Kidnaping is suspected.

December 25: Sis returns to U.S.

1985
January 8: Father Lawrence Martin Jenco, head of Roman Catholic Relief Services in Lebanon, is kidnaped.

Early January: Jesse Jackson embarks on an overseas mission on Jerry's behalf. He returns a few days later saying that his contacts told him his trip is premature.

February 14: Syrian soldiers find Jerry at about 2 A.M. hiding beneath a truck early in the morning alongside the main Bekaa Valley highway running through Baalbeck.

February 15: Jerry and Sis are reunited at Rhine Main airport, Frankfurt, West Germany.

March 16: Associated Press Mideast Bureau Chief Terry Anderson is kidnaped.

May 28: David Jacobsen, American University of Beirut Hospital administrator, is kidnaped.

June 3: William Buckley dies in captivity. His death is made public by his captors on October 4.

June 9: American University of Beirut Acting Dean of Agriculture Thomas Sutherland is kidnaped.

Mid-July: American Hostage Committee is formed.

September 14: Benjamin Weir is released and flown to the U.S.

October 29: American Hostage Committee granted a closed hearing with the House Foreign Affairs Committee. The same day an editorial in the *New York Post,* falsely accusing the committee of being pawns of the PLO, leads to its eventual disbanding.

1986
April 17: Hostage Peter Kilburn murdered in response to U.S. bombing of Libya the previous Monday. Two British hostages and British-American journalist Alec Collett are murdered for the same reason.

July 26: Lawrence Martin Jenco is freed.

September 9: Frank Reed, director of the Lebanon International School, is kidnaped.

September 12: Joseph Cicippio, acting comptroller of the American

University of Beirut, is kidnaped.

October 21: Children's book author Edward Austin Tracy is kidnaped.

November 2: David Jacobsen is freed. Within a month the release of Jacobsen, Jenco and Weir is connected with the "Iran-Contra" sale of military weapons to Iran—the sale profits financing the secret, unlawful purchase of arms for Nicaraguan Contras.

1987

January 20: Terry Waite, the Anglican archbishop of Canterbury's hostage negotiator, disappears. He probably has been kidnaped. Waite had publicly implied that he had played a crucial role in the release of hostages Weir, Jenco and Jacobsen. That apparently led to the loss of his credibility with the captors who knew better. When his close contacts with Iran-Contra mastermind, U.S. Marine Lt. Colonel Oliver North were revealed, he apparently lost their trust too.

January 24: Beirut University College educators Robert Polhill, Alann Steen and Jesse Turner are kidnaped.

May 5: Iran-Contra congressional investigation hearings begin.

June 17: ABC-TV newsman Charles Glass is kidnaped. He escapes or is released two months later, on August 18.

1988

February 17: Marine Lt. Col. William Higgins is taken prisoner in southern Lebanon, where he was heading a UN observer group attached to the UN Lebanese peace-keeping force.

1989

July 31: The captors of Lt. Col. Higgins announce they have hanged him in retaliation for the kidnaping of Sheik Abdul Karim Obeid. Three days earlier there is speculation that he actually may have died or been killed by his captors some time before then.